THE WYCHE WAY
by Guy Vowles

CW00376849

CONTENTS

Acknowledgements

As I mention in my introduction, this trail would not have been possible without the original idea formulated by Fred Wood, who was a great force in Gloucestershire walking in the 1970's and 80's. Likewise John White, also of The Cheltenham Rambling Club, who had the foresight to keep all the original programmes, with the necessary details to make it possible.

There have been a number of other Cheltenham Rambling Club members who have helped with the many walkovers and in particular Jim Mason's thoughtful and experienced help has been much appreciated.

Once again, Geoff Gwatkin has provided the hand drawn maps which so enhance the book.

I am also very grateful to Eric Holloway at Typecraft, who remained unflustered by my many changes, and who has made several worthwhile suggestions for improving the layout of the book.

Lastly, but certainly not least, I am very indebted to my wife Linetha, who could not originally understand why I should consider writing yet another book, but then gave her full hearted support, provided it was definitely my last one!

INTRODUCTION

What's in a Name?

Nearly all of the many long distance paths in the UK can be slotted into definite styles so that for topographical, an example might well be The Greensands Way, The Beacons Way, or The Cotswold Way. There are also many boundary walks like The Ross Round or The Gloucestershire Way and then there are also historical trails like Lady Anne's Way and St Cuthberts Way. There is even an architectural trail, The Palladian Way, but where does The Wyche Way fit in?

I have to confess straight away that it was not my original idea. It was thought up by Fred Wood who was a prominent Gloucestershire rambler and The Leader for Cheltenham Rambling Club in the late 1970's. He devised it as a series of circular walks that started outside Broadway and finished at Kington thereby linking up The Cotswold Way and The Offa's Dyke path. Both these trails were then in their infancy so it was quite an innovative idea at the time. It did, however, take nearly four years for him to work out the route and to walk it with Cheltenham Rambling Club. I was also lucky enough to meet a member of the club, John White, who not only remembered the walks, but who also had in his possession all the original programmes with brief route descriptions. Fred had worked out the title from several points of interest.

Firstly, the route was to pass through The Wyche Cutting outside Malvern. Secondly, there was the direction to either The Cotswold Way or Offa's Dyke ie Which Way, and lastly he discovered old cottages by the church in Kington with a number of Wych related names.

Planning The Route

Once I had John's CRC programmes I was able to mark up the OS maps with places mentioned and then to plan an embryo route for a linear long distance walk. This originally worked out at just over 110km (70 miles) so I thought that it would divide quite nicely into six stages and I then started looking at suitable starting and finishing points for each stage. It was at this juncture that I realized that the walk would be rather better if it was reversed and started at Kington since the flatter half of the walk would then be in the first three days and would lead up to The Malvern Hills, then Bredon Hill, and culminate at Broadway Tower. Many walkers might also be travelling back to London and the home counties, which would be easier with a Broadway finish.

Fine Tuning The Route

Nearly all local walk leaders do a walkover and for a linear walk it is even more important but you do also need good and useful companions. I had only just met Jim Mason before this walk but his help has been immeasurable. Firstly, Jim is a councillor in Winchcombe and has been responsible for furthering the town's 'Walkers are Welcome' status and indeed they also have their own very successful LD trail - The Winchcombe Way. Jim was enthusiastic about the project from the very start and the first of our many coincidences was to find out that Kington also had 'Walkers are Welcome' status. The local walking committee now see their town as a focal point for Herefordshire walking with six long distance trails already passing through the town, in addition to this one.

We had to do three walkovers for the first easy stage through to the very attractive 'Black and White' village of Weobley but received the first of many helpful bits of advice when we were told of a discretionary route that enabled us to avoid several miles of road walking. The rest of the six stages went well and in the summer of 2013 we walked the whole route with CRC where we received very good support with an average of over 20 members on each stage. We were able to provide them with a pub stop on four of the stages and we managed a tea stop after every stage so it proved to be a very social and well received walk.

Distances, measured with GPS, do tend to creep up over the original estimates, and Stage 4 which was due to start from Fromes Hill, finished at Upton upon Severn, which with the climb over the Malverns, turned out to be an overlong and rather tough stage at about 27km (17miles). We had quite a chat about this and decided to put in an extra stage whereby Stage 3 would be shortened and finish at the attractive Bishops Frome village, which has more facilities. We would then take Stage 4 over North Hill and finish in the centre of Malvern. This has the added addition of a main line rail station so that walkers could divide the overall walk into four and then a later three stages. Fit long distance walkers could still do the original long stage, bypassing Malvern, but otherwise Stage 5 now goes back over the Malverns, passes through The Wyche, with it's pub of the same name, and finishes as previously at Upton on Severn.

The last two stages are as originally planned but the 7 stages now take the overall distance up to about 130km (80 miles) with a reasonable average of just under 20km (12miles) per day.

The Walking
I prefer to show the walking distances in kilometres and it is also much more convenient and accurate to mention smaller distances in metres rather than fractions of a mile. An easy walking pace is 4km an hour (2.5 MPH) which is a kilometre every quarter of an hour. This is also easy to equate with distance squares on an OS map, and rather like motoring on

the continent, kilometres pass more quickly than miles. My approximate walking times do not include for any stops and are based on between 4 and 5 km an hour.

This should prove to be quite a sociable walk for most participants and nearly every stage finishes at a main road or village where there is accommodation and local transport. After two days walkers will see The Malverns in the distance and thereafter the route passes through a fascinating contrast of different countryside but with quite a few climbs.

The hand drawn maps for this book are all based on the OS Landranger series and whilst these plus the script and the distinctive way marking may be adequate it is recommended that walkers also carry the more detailed Explorer maps for the route. The necessary map numbers are shown at the start of each stage.

Across Two Countries?

Purchasers of this book will have no doubt already noticed that the map on the back cover shows not only The Wyche Way but also a connecting route using mainly other LD trails that could provide a unique long distance route between Aberystwth and London.

I normally provide an overall map to show how a route is located nationally and in this instance I was talking to a friend about walking The Wye Valley Way when it dawned on me, that with a little extra input, it could be joined on to meet The Wyche Way, and that from Broadway, it would once again need little effort to continue on to Chipping Campden (the start of The Cotswold Way) and then on to Little Rollright, to join The Shakespeare Way all the way down to London. So, in the last chapter of the book we are showing my idea for those extra unofficial bits that are required to make up the whole route and the mileage chart for this whole long mega route which of course can all be done separately.

This way, walkers could have a week on The Wyche Way, a week or so walking from Aberyswyth to Kington, and then maybe a week or more walking from Broadway to London. All very approximate and dependant on a walker's ability, but food for thought and maybe dreams!

STAGES
Distances and Ascent

CUMULATIVE ASCENT

STAGE 1
Kington - Weobley   **18km** (11.25m)

STAGE 2
Weobley - Bodenham   **17km** (10.6m)

STAGE 3
Bodenham - Bishops Frome   **19km** (11.88m)

STAGE 4
Bishops Frome - Malvern   **16km** (10.00m)

STAGE 5
Malvern – Upton upon Severn   **17km** (10.6m)

STAGE 6
Upton upon Severn - Ashton u Hill **22km** (13.75m)

STAGE 7
Ashton under Hill -Broadway Tower **17km** (10.6m)

_____

TOTALS   **126km** (78.75m)

STAGE 1	**190m** (623 ft)	
STAGE 2	**200m** (656 ft)	
STAGE 3	**234m** (770 ft)	
STAGE 4	**664m** (2175 ft)	
STAGE 5	**361m** (1150 ft)	
STAGE 6	**411m** (1348 ft)	
STAGE 7	**401m** (1315 ft)	

TOTALS   **2461m** (8072 ft)

KINGTON

Walking The Herefordshire Trail a few years ago was an enjoyable and interesting experience, that was heightened by the contrast in the five market towns we visited , of which Kington, at under 3000 population, is the smallest. They all have different attributes but from a walking perspective Kington stands alone. It has more long distance paths converging on a town of it's size, than anywhere else in the UK. I also discovered on their new walking festival that it is possible to do a demanding and really good local 24km (15 mile) walk that takes in eight surrounding hills all over 300m (1000 feet). The 'Walkers are Welcome' initiative which the town offers is not just a promise.

It is also the remotest of the Herefordshire market towns and one gets a definite feel that you are almost in Wales. Despite it's size, the town has all the facilities one could want, with plenty of accommodation from it's two hotels and several good and contrasting pubs as well as quite a few B&B's and also a youth hostel. There is a small Tourist information office and lots of different little, old fashioned, shops that offer good personal service.

I have been visiting Kington for more years than I care to remember and hope to be enjoying many more visits in the future. It is a very fitting place to start or to join a long distance trail.

LONG DISTANCE TRAILS THROUGH KINGTON

The Offa's Dyke Path *(Chepstow to Prestatyn)*	177 miles
The Herefordshire Trail *(Circular from Ledbury)*	154 miles
The Wyche Way *(Kington to Broadway Tower)*	**79 miles**
Black and White Villages Trail *(Circular from Leominster)*	43 miles
The Arrow Valley Trail *(Gwaencester Hill to Leominster)*	35 miles
The Mortimer Trail *(Ludlow to Kington)*	30 miles
Vaughan's Way *(Kington to Bredwerdine)*	17 miles

TRANSPORT CONNECTIONS

Train - Nearest station Leominster (12miles) Arriva Wales Cardiff & Shrewsbury line.
- Hereford (20miles) First Great Western
- London - Worcester - Birmingham line

Long Distance Coach -
National Express No44 - London Victoria - Heathrow - Oxford - Cheltenham - Gloucester - Ross on Wye - Hereford

Local Bus service
Hereford to Llandrindod Wells (Sargents) No 461/462 Mon - Sat hourly Leominster No 493 not so frequent.

Weobley from the castle site

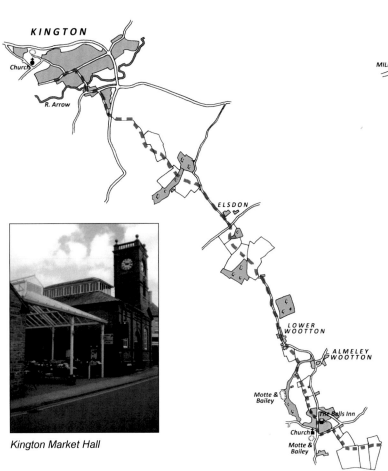

KINGTON

Church

R. Arrow

ELSDON

LOWER
WOOTTON

ALMELEY
WOOTTON

Motte &
Bailey

The Bells Inn

Church

Motte &
Bailey

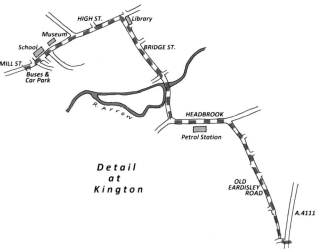

HIGH ST.

Library

Museum

BRIDGE ST.

School

MILL ST.

Buses &
Car Park

R. Arrow

HEADBROOK

Petrol Station

Detail
at
Kington

OLD
EARDISLEY
ROAD

A.4111

Kington Market Hall

The Bells Inn, Almeley

THE WYCHE WAY

STAGE 1 – Kington to Weobley
18.0km (11.25m) Allow 4 -5 hours without stops

This is an easygoing and mainly flat stage through typical agricultural countryside, with a good early stop possible at Almeley. The highlight of the day's walking is when the ancient and 'timbered' house, The Ley, is reached just before Weobley.

The walk starts from the Mill Street car park which is adjacent to the town centre bus stop. Turn right, pass the Burton Hotel and at the road junction continue ahead into The High Street. After 200m turn right into Bridge Street and leave the town as you cross the bridge over the River Arrow. Shortly after the road becomes Headbrook, but continue on past a filling station to take a turning on the right SP Old Eardisley Road, and continue up to the end of the road where it becomes a track. **(1km)**

Arrive at a main road and cross over carefully to a stile with a gate alongside. Bear right in the field and walk down over rough ground to reach a footbridge over a stream. In the next field (can be crops) continue straight ahead up the incline, heading to the right of Oak trees on the far side. Arrive at a hedge and walk left up to the corner of the field to find a stile

and pedestrian gate with the first sign for Vaughan's Way which we shall follow most of the way to Almeley. Continue in the next field, with the hedge on your left, on a wide grass margin. In the next field and after 200m, turn left, and walk up to a stile in the hedge opposite. **(2km)**

Over the stile, the route proceeds in a diagonal line up to the top right hand corner of the field but if the field is in crop it may be better to walk straight across the field and then follow the hedge and narrow border up to the stile in the corner. Continue ahead in the next field still following the boundary hedge on the left to reach another stile at the bottom of the field and then walk on up towards a band of woodland. Just before this, is a good spot for a rest, with maybe some refreshment, and a chance to look back on your progress, with a superb view of Kington nestling between the surrounding hills. Cross a stile into the woodland and pass through it to another stile on the far side. Continue on over further stiles on either side of an access road and then continue down to a gateway to the left of farm buildings. **(3km)** Turn right on the lane and follow it for 500m down to a T junction. Cross a stile immediately opposite and bear right to walk down through pasture to the right of a lake. Ascend up to a gateway and then continue on down, over a stile, to a gate at the edge of woodland. **(4km)**

The line for the footpath is then diagonally right to the corner with buildings beyond but if the field is in crop, or it is waterlogged, it may be easier to walk around the field on the right hand side and to then join a farm track up to the farm. Walk up to the farm entrance, turn right onto the access road, and follow it for a kilometre to Lower Wootton. (**5km** midway on road)

Follow the road as it bears left after farm buildings where you will see a FP sign in the hedge on the right. Cross a stile and proceed half left in the field to find a stile and a pedestrian gate in the far corner by an Oak tree. Turn right in the next field and walk to a stile, where continue on down a steep path to a sunken track with a deep stream beyond. (**6km**)

Turn right and walk along the track for 100m, but then cross the stream on a footbridge and ascend up the steep bank on the other side. Bear right across the field to the top left corner with a stile. Walk across to the corner of the next field and continue ahead towards the buildings of Almeley with a fence on the right. Cross over two more stiles to arrive on a minor estate road in the village (**7km**) and follow this road around to arrive at a larger road where turn right and walk down to The Bells Inn. (**7.5km**) This basic little village Inn has recently had a bit of a make-over and the landlord and his wife have converted the old lounge bar into a well stocked shop with all sorts of foodstuffs and many other useful items. Consequently the shop and the pub are open all day and every day which is really enterprising, and will hopefully prove to be indispensable for the villagers and hungry walkers!

Continue down the road from the pub, past the church and take a left turning SP Woonton and Weobley. After 200m turn right off the road (**8km**) and pass through a gate (stile obscured) into a field where follow the right hand boundary down to a high level double stile. Continue in the next field on the same line and reach a pair of stiles to the left of a gate.

Turn left in the next field and follow the hedge to a metal gate. Continue on the same line to a further gate. In the next field pass over the brow of the field and drop down to a stile and footbridge over a stream.(**9km**) Initially bear left in the next field up to the boundary fence, which follow down to a muddy area with an obvious double track beyond. Follow this track up to lane where continue straight on ahead to a junction. Turn right and follow the road as it soon bears left and then right.

Continue down, the now straight road, past a large complex of farm buildings (**10km**) to pass Newchurch Farm after a further 500m. Soon after, at a sharp right hand bend, turn off left into the large field opposite and make your way, past a lone Oak tree in the middle of the field to a gap in the far boundary (about 200m to the left of a prominent farmhouse). Drop down to cross a muddy area with a planked bridge and make your way up towards a farmhouse. The unmarked route is then through a stockade of post and rail fencing with the gates tied up. Arrive at the busy main road outside and initially turn left but then, almost immediately right, onto a track to Park Farm. (**11km**)

After 200m bear off to the left and follow the bridleway alongside the hedge, though two gates, and then bear right just before the next hedge to find another gate with a bridleway on the other side. (**12km**)

Turn left on the grassy margin but after 50m bear right across the field and make for the woodland opposite. Cross a small footbridge, and continue alongside the woodland to reach a stile and a minor road.(**13km**) Turn right and walk for 100m where turn left up the drive to Hyatt Sarnesfield farm where the track now becomes a permissive right of way. (**14km**) Continue past a nice stone cottage and after 100m turn left onto a footpath with an attractive avenue of trees ahead. Pass the trees and arrive at a field junction with a stile and way marking signs but continue straight ahead with farm buildings visible up ahead.(**15km**) Cross a footbridge, pass through a gate and continue on the same line up towards the farm.

Bear left past the farm buildings and pass through several lots of gates to emerge on the other side in front of The Ley, which must be, one of the finest examples of a very old (Elizabethan origins) timbered farmhouse. (**16km**)

Just beyond the house and past a pond on the left there is a small wooden gate, where cross a small piece of pasture to another gate. Continue with the hedge on the right and notice the fine spire of Weobley Church in the distance. Pass through a kissing gate and proceed up to another kissing gate but before this, turn sharp right and walk down (50m) to a further gate. (**17km**) Pass through this one, and cross a narrow field to another gate. In the next field (may have crops) turn right to another gate visible in the far hedge.

Cross a lane carefully and go through another gate into a field where turn left and pass by venerable Oak

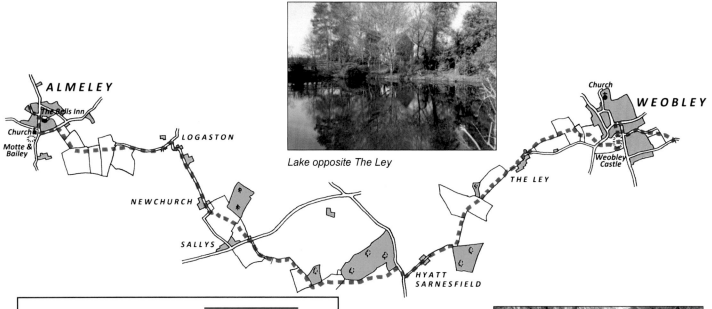

ALMELEY

The Bells Inn

Church

Motte & Bailey

LOGASTON

NEWCHURCH

SALLYS

HYATT SARNESFIELD

Lake opposite The Ley

THE LEY

Church

WEOBLEY

Weobley Castle

Mellington House
Weobley

Mellington House B&B apartments are situated right in the centre of the delightful black and white timbered village of Weobley.

Good local walks, shops, tearoom, Post Office, excellent restaurants and a lovely historic inn are all nearby.

Double and Twin rooms, Full English Breakfast, Garden, TV, DVD, wifi, kitchen facilities.

Mellington House, Broad Street, Weobley, Herefordshire. HR4 8SA
Chris and Alison Saunders: Tel:- 01544 318537
email:- info@mellingtonhouse.co.uk Website:- www.mellingtonhouse.co.uk

Approaching Weobley Castle

trees and arrive at a footbridge in the hedge. After another gate, make your way up onto a knoll which is all that remains of Weobley Castle. No doubt most of the stone found it's way into the older cottages in the village.

Turn left and walk down towards the village past a line of Oaks and pass an information board showing all the history of the castle. Continue on though an old metal gate and emerge at the top of this most attractive village. (**18km**)

THE BLACK AND WHITE VILLAGE TRAIL AND WEOBLEY

The original trail, which was designed for motorists, is based on 11 villages around Kington and Leominster. These are Dilwyn, Sarnesfield, Kinnersley, Eardisley, Lyonshall. Pembridge, Eardisland, Kingsland, Yarpole, Wigmore and Weobley. There are many pockets of black and white timbered buildings in England but this must represent the largest concentration in any one area. All of them have their charm, but to my mind, the most impressive are Pembridge and Weobley. The main street of Pembridge is certainly spectacular but for all round facilities, as well as the architecture, Weobley may have the advantage, and not for nothing, has it twice been voted in the top ten villages in the country. Up until the early 19th century it was a borough and returned two members to parliament, but the later decline in agricultural trade found many villages with declining population.

Weobley still has two pubs, a nice little variety of independent shops including a good butcher, a delicatessen with high quality tea shop, and last, but not least, for tired walkers, quite a few B&B establishments. It is definitely worth while taking a stroll around the village to see all the ancient houses, some of which date back to the 15th century, and also to visit the fine church, which has the second highest spire in Herefordshire. The Hereford to Kington bus passes through the village nearly every hour.

The Ley - medieval origins

Magpie sculpture, Weobley

WEOBLEY

Church

Weobley Castle

MEERS PLACE

KINGS PYON

Church

BUSH BANK

BRICK HOUSE

CANON PYON HOUSE

A.4110

Westhope Wood

WESTHOPE HILL

Weobley High Street

THE WYCHE WAY

STAGE 2 – Weobley to Bodenham

(OS Explorer map 202)

17.0km (10.63m) Allow 4-5 hours walking without stops

This is another easy going stage. There is one gradual ascent in the morning up to Westhope Common and then there are two fine, long ridges, with superb views, both before and after a good lunchtime stop at the Queens Wood Country Park.

At the top of the village, where you arrived from the castle, turn left into The High Street, pass The Unicorn Inn, and then turn right SP Kings Pyon and Wormsley. After 200m turn left SP Burton Gardens along an enclosed footpath which leads to a modern development of houses and bungalows. Continue on the same line, past the houses, to find a gap in the fencing in the top left hand corner. Turn right on the grassy track and after 200m fork left and continue up to a kissing gate. After this, fork left across the field to another similar gate and continue across the next field to another gate in the corner with a lane beyond. **(1km)**

Cross the road to another gate and continue ahead on the enclosed path, through the next field, with the hedge on the right, to another gate at the bottom of the field. Continue across a narrow field, through another gate, to cross a further field, on the same line making for a red brick cottage ahead. Arrive at a stile to the right of the cottage with a lane beyond. **(2km)**

Cross the lane and stile on the other side, and bear right across the field to find a stile in the opposite hedge, which is to the left of a large modern house. In the next field take the left hand footpath which follows the hedge on the left through two fields to the farm buildings of Meers Place. Pass through three metal farm gates, and exit from the farmyard on the access track, which leads up to a minor road. **(3km)**

Turn right on the road and follow it for a km to reach a T junction **(4km)** where turn right. After 50m turn left through double gates into a field. (Walkers with a love of fine churches, and with time to spare, might consider a small detour, by continuing along the road, (300m) to view St Mary's church in the attractive village of Kings Pyon, which also makes a nice spot for a morning refreshment break.)

The main route continues alongside an orchard, arrives at a stile, and then forks right in the next field to arrive at a gateway with a lane beyond. Turn left on the lane and proceed for 300m where turn off right onto a bridle path. Pass through two fields **(5km)** to arrive alongside Brick House where join a large track and turn left. Walk past the farm buildings and continue all the way up the access road to reach a main road. **(6km)**

Turn right and then almost immediately left, SP Westhope. After 50m turn left off the road, and proceed alongside farm buildings. Pass through a metal gate, bear right into the adjoining field, and continue through an open gateway up towards the woodland ahead. Arrive at the edge of the woodland where turn right and follow the fence up to a stile in the top corner of the field. **(7km)**

Cross the stile and follow the path in the wood as it gently rises. Arrive at a junction, turn right and continue climbing. Arrive at another junction where turn left and then after 50m turn right to ascend up to wooden gate alongside a metal gate. Turn right and follow the hedge on the right through two fields, where you are now on Westhope Common with great views over to Hay Bluff in the west.

Arrive at a gate **(8km)** with a vehicular track beyond which cross and take the track opposite by a neighbourhood watch sign. After farm buildings the track becomes narrower and leads on to another track where cross to another vehicular track. This passes several houses but do not divert off the main track, and emerge into open countryside with more fantastic

views on either side. Arrive at a gateway where soon after bear left past a pond and across the field to find a hidden stile in the opposite hedgerow.

Continue half right across the next field to arrive at another stile **(9km)** where turn right and follow the hedge. Pass through a metal gate and then bear slightly right and proceed up to a gateway alongside the hedge in the distance. Continue ahead through two more gates, cross the middle of the next field heading for another gate. **(10km)**

Pass through another gate and arrive on a surfaced track which follow through another gate and reach a concreted area, which cross and pass through two more gates in close proximity. In the next large field the route is diagonally right to the far corner where reach a tarmac estate road. **(11km)** Turn left and walk for 200m to reach rather nice wooden gates with a stile to the right. Continue ahead on the road past a portable building business. Bear left at a fork and then left again at a T junction. Turn left and walk down the hill for 300m, and then opposite a track on the left, turn right into the wood by a telegraph pole. **(12km)** Follow the track ahead into the wood and at the top cross another track, where soon after bear right by a timber barrier and continue ahead towards the main buildings of the Country park. **(12.6km)**

You will see that there are plenty of picnic tables scattered around the vicinity on which you can either enjoy your own picnic lunch, or there is a very good and reasonably priced café which is also next door to an information centre (presently closed). Part of the extensive woodland has been designated as an arboretum where there is much to admire.

After your refreshment the route continues from the red telephone box, outside the information centre, where turn left and walk away from the buildings on the access road. Soon arrive alongside the main road and turn left along the grass verge, where after 50m you will see a stone memorial on your left.

This commemorated the date in 1935 when the land was donated by Herefordshire County Council and Queen Mary, the wife of George 5th, officially opened the facility as a public park. Subsequently, our present Queen returned in 1957 to plant a commemorative tree. It is certainly rewarding that the country park continues to be so very well used today.

Cross the busy main road carefully (blind corner) opposite the memorial, and enter the woodland through a pedestrian gate. The narrow path winds through the wood **(13km)** to arrive at a junction, where turn right on the wider track. Arrive at another junction and continue ahead to a gate with open countryside beyond with more lovely views on both sides. Continue ahead on the surfaced track towards farm buildings in the distance **(14km)** and pass through a gateway and past the buildings. Cross a cattle grid and continue ahead on a grassy track with an avenue of chestnut and beech trees on the right.

Arrive at another cattle grid, turn right and walk along the edge of the woodland following the track across the field, past fine oak trees towards a wooden gate ahead. **(15km)** Pass through two more gates with the first views of The Malverns in the far distance. Drop down on rough ground under trees to another gate where the path becomes a sunken way. The large village of Bodenham is now visible below but beyond the last gate it is preferable to climb up the bank on the right, rather than follow the sunken way, and then to walk down the field to a metal gate in the bottom left hand corner of the field.

The sunken path is now enclosed between tall hedges and is rather attractive and private as it descends to houses to reach an access track, where turn right, and then reach a minor road. **(16km)** Turn left and soon cross quite a substantial bridge over the River Lugg. Cross another small bridge, where soon after there is a footpath to the right, which could enable walkers, not stopping in Bodenham, to cut across the south of the village and join the onward route for the

Queens Wood Country Park

Englands Gate Pub

WESTHOPE HILL

Friars Grove

KIPPERKNOWLE

HAMPTON COURT

DINMORE HILL

Queens Wood Country Park

HENHOUSE

BODENHAM

Church

A.49

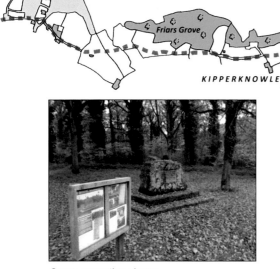

Commemorative plaque

next stage. Please note that this diversion is not way marked. Otherwise continue along the road, fork right at the next junction now following a stream on the right, and arrive in the village at a T junction with the attractive Englands Gate pub to the left. **(17km)**

Bodenham and Englands Gate

This large village is almost equidistant (9 miles) between Hereford and Leominster and there is a regular bus service to the latter large market town, which is also served by main line railway. The Englands Gate Pub, which has 16th century origins, may have been named when the Welsh border was not so far west as it is today and when this place was actually quite near the border. The large pub has plenty of accommodation with an overflow into the converted barn alongside. They have comprehensive menus and are open all day at weekends.

Just a few hundred metres along the main road (A417) in the Ledbury direction is also a golf club with good catering facilities, which is open to the public. This is another alternative to the pub, and possibly better for Tea at the end of the day.

A pub no longer

An old Roman road

Wood carving at Moreton Wood

THE WYCHE WAY

STAGE 3 – Bodenham to Bishops Frome
(OS Explorer map 202)
19km (11.88m) Allow 5-6 hours without stops

This is the last of the flatter stages before the main hills. There are not many footpaths available in the desired easterly direction so that there is quite a lot of (quiet) lane walking on this stage. There are several points of interest with an unknown Roman road and an innovative woodland operation on the route. The Malverns are getting distinctly nearer.

Turn right outside The England's Gate pub and walk down the main street of the village for 500m and take an enclosed footpath on the left that leads up to a stile and a field beyond. Cross another stile and then bear right across a field to a gate that is to the left of farm buildings. Pass through a pedestrian gate to arrive on a minor road where turn left, and walk along it for another 500m. (1km halfway along the road)

Turn right off the road, before some substantial steel clad barns, on a rough surfaced bridleway. Follow the hedge on the right until the bridleway arrives alongside houses and the surface becomes tarmac. **(2km)** Pass a number of interesting houses, until almost up to a main road and by a post box turn right on to a minor road. Follow this for a kilometre to a junction **(3km)** and fork left. The hamlets here are all called Maunds and just before you reach the third one and Upper Maund Farm, turn right off the lane and cross a gate into a field.

Continue up the field, keeping close to the hedge on the right but at the top veer slightly left to find a stile in a recess. **(4km)** On the other side of the stile is a wide well maintained bridleway where turn left. This is now the route of The Three Rivers long distance riding trail which starts near Clifton on Teme in Worcestershire and ends after 95 miles near Brecon. This part of the bridleway was also a Roman road which probably came from Alcester and continued down towards the Roman fort at Kenchester near Hereford.

Follow the bridleway for nearly a kilometre to reach a minor road **(5km)** and turn left. Reach a T junction with a former pub on the left and continue straight ahead for 200m to reach the busy A417 Leominster – Ledbury road. Cross over carefully onto a minor road SP Little Cowerne.

The route winds along past a number of attractive houses, continues straight ahead at a road junction, **(6km)** and then bears left uphill at the next junction to pass a telephone box with a conveniently placed bench for a mid morning break. Continue on the road past fishing pools on the right and then start ascending up towards a band of woodland. Just before the top, turn right onto a surfaced track, **(7km)** which after 400m, becomes tarmac and is an access road to a property called Dovedale. Continue on a footpath into Moreton Wood, which a couple have recently purchased, and where they have set up a woodland enterprise with some manufacturing of timber based products. They also organize courses on coppicing and woodland management. Anyone who is interested in more details or a guided tour can contact them on 07929 851674

The footpath bears left before their workshop, and continues down through the wood to emerge at the bottom with a large field on the left **(8km)**.The route is straight across it and on a line towards distant houses on a ridge but if the field is in crop or waterlogged it may be better to walk around the left hand side. Arrive at the other side and bear slightly right to cross a flat bridge over a wide ditch between two fields. The way ahead up to the ridge can be seen quite clearly but rather than taking a direct line it may be better to walk up the right hand border. At the end of the next field the route is straight across to the corner of the hedge opposite **(9km)** where a prominent track leads up towards the houses on the ridge.

Arrive at an open gateway with a major road beyond.

Turn right and walk down to the next corner where the post office and stores is presently open but up for sale. Turn left SP Bishops Frome & Much Cowerne and walk down the minor road **(10km)** past a variety of different properties with good views to the left. After about 600m turn right on a track just past Pumpkin Cottage which is a nice half timbered property. After 60m turn left **(11km)** onto an enclosed path with two stiles and emerge into a field. Bear right to find another stile in the top right hand corner which cross and turn sharp left. Cross an access track to the large farmhouse on the left and continue ahead following the left hand boundary with a view of Much Cowerne church ahead.

Continue following the hedge around the bottom of the field until a stile is reached. Bear half right in the next narrow field towards the church, and find a planked bridge **(12km)** (initially hidden) over a stream and continue up to a small metal gate that gives access to the churchyard. Bear left and walk over the rough grass to the more formal area. St Mary's church is quite large with some old tombs and one suspects that the congregation was considerably larger in times past.

Leave the churchyard through the double wooden gates opposite the notice board and bear left following the main driveway out. An interesting building is seen on the right, which almost looks like an old railway station, but judging from the construction, it may have been a drying warehouse for hops. There is further confusion at the end of the drive where there are two parallel roads, just a few metres apart, that lead out to a minor road. I guess that the road leading to the farm buildings was originally private and that a separate road was put in for access to the church.

Arrive at a road junction and cross straight over soon passing an impressive old school on the right. After about 300m arrive at a (locked) metal gate on the left and cross this into a field of Christmas trees. Walk up on the right hand side of the hedge for about 200m and then turn right on a broad track, between the trees, down to the bottom of the field where there is a bridge over a stream (actually the River Lodon) which is where you join The Three Choirs Way. **(13km)**

The Three Choirs Way
This is a 100 mile circular trail that connects up the three cities which organize the famous musical festival of the same name. The route is described as starting from Gloucester and then passing through west Gloucestershire to Hereford. It then turns back towards Worcester, where we follow it for a little while around Much Cowerne. From Worcester, it proceeds south west to Malvern, and back to Gloucester via the Malvern Hills. The author managed some years

ago to stop off on the way, outside Worcester, to visit the Elgar centre, which was very atmospheric with some of Elgar's best known music playing in the background.

Cross a broken stile over the stream and follow the boundary fence and hedge on the right through four fields, with often muddy gateways, to arrive alongside Hope's Rough Farm. **(14km)** Continue past the farm and then walk down between the farm and other buildings to find a gate onto an access track. Turn left and walk up to a road junction.

There is now a choice of routes to Bishops Frome. The shortest route to the left, (one kilometre less) is all road, very boring and not worthwhile, unless time is pressing or the weather is very bad. Our preferred, and more attractive, route is to the right where continue up a No Through Road, and just before the gateway to a house, find a stile on the right that gives access to a small ornamental garden. **(15km)**

Through an ornamental garden

Christmas trees

A.465

BURLEY
GATE

WYNN'S
GREEN

Church

MUCH
COWARNE

HOPES
ROUGH

BROMTREES
HALL

LOWER
WALTON

FIVE
BRIDGES

FROGEND

A.4103

BISHOPS
FROME

Church

CHEYNEY
COURT

The Hop
Pocket

NEW HOUSE

Much Cowerne church

Pass diagonally through the garden to find a stile on the far side, where turn left in the next field and walk up to a kissing gate. Pass through this and another one shortly after. The route now follows the left hand boundary hedge through several orchards and some rather nice Oak woodland.

Arrive at an open gateway, **(16km)** ignore a footpath sign to the right, and continue ahead on the same line over a small bridge and stile. In the next field, soon spot a stile on the left and cross this and drop down to a wide sunken track where turn right. Follow this through metal gates, where it becomes surfaced and leads down to the busy A4103 Worcester to Hereford road. **(17km)**
(Please be warned that the sunken track can get quite overgrown and also be boggy so that it is also possible to continue alongside the hedge and join the end of the sunken track some 400m later although this alternative is not an official footpath)

Turn left on the grass verge, and then almost immediately turn left again, to pass over a metal gate into a long field. Cross over to the far side and find a stile 20 metres in from the right hand corner. The next field can be in crop and it may be necessary to walk around the right hand boundary but otherwise continue straight across to find a gap in the hedge on the far side to the right of a tree.

Turn right and emerge on a minor road **(18km)** where 300m to the right, is The Hop Pocket Farm shop, with a café and all sorts of different merchandise, but we turn left for a few metres and then cross over the road to a gap into a field. Walk quite close to the hedge and stream on the right, to arrive at a stile in the far hedge, with a lane beyond. The next 800m is repeated on the next stage so that walkers, who are not staying in Bishops Frome, or are on a different schedule, do not need to walk this section. However we shall describe the route in both directions.

Cross a stile on the opposite side of the lane and note that you have just joined The Herefordshire Trail. Follow the well trodden path around the field, alongside the infant river Frome and at the end of the field turn sharp left and head for the church. Notice the rather imposing old red brick house on the left, which may have been the original rectory.

Pass through a wooden kissing gate, and just past the church, take a right fork which leads you out through the imposing lych gate into the centre of this attractive village. **(19km)**

BISHOPS FROME
One must assume that at some stage there was an ecclesiastical connection for the name but certainly the second part is taken from the river that runs

through the village and joins the River Severn near Worcester. Despite being five miles from the nearest town, (Bromyard) the village is quite self sufficient. It has two good pubs of which The Chase has accommodation whilst the Green Dragon presently has a great selection of real ales and ciders. There is a large modern hall known as The Village Centre and this has an adjoining small shop, manned by volunteers, that has most essentials. There is also the aforementioned Hop Pocket store about 1km south.

Cheyney Mill Stage 4

BISHOPS FROME

Church

CHEYNEY COURT

FROMES HILL

WOODCROFT FARMS

HILL FARM

Beacon Hill

HOLLINGS HILL

ROOK ROW

MOOREND COURT

Church

MATHON

Mathon Church

Cheyney Court Gardens

32

THE WYCHE WAY

STAGE 4 – Bishops Frome to Great Malvern
(OS Explorer maps 202 & 190)
19km (11.88m) Allow 5-6 hours walking

This is probably the toughest stage on the whole trail with three major climbs, lots of interesting woodland and good views. There is regrettably no pub on the route but there is a shop, with a cafe, just before the last climb.

From the centre of the village, and outside The Chase Inn, turn right and walk down the pavement towards the church. Pass through the ornamental lych gate and continue on the footpath past the main door to arrive at another small gate on the far side of the churchyard. Continue through a small field to a crossing track with a bridge opposite.(note that you are now following The Herefordshire Trail for the next three kilometres to Fromes Hill)

THE HEREFORDSHIRE TRAIL
This is a circular 154 mile walk around the county that was organized by Herefordshire Ramblers some ten years ago. The official route starts at Ledbury, which is probably the most attractive market town in the county, and then continues on to Ross on Wye. It passes quite close to Hay on Wye, which is just in Wales, before continuing up to Kington. It then proceeds up to the far north of the county, and just south of Ludlow, which is in Shropshire, before descending down to Leominster, which is the largest market town in the county. It then continues on down to Bromyard and finally back to Ledbury. It is a very varied and quite challenging trail since there are a great number of stiles, of which many are double ones at either end of bridges. There are many fine buildings to admire, and when walking the trail with Cheltenham Ramblers we nearly always managed a mid morning break in one of the many fascinating old churches, which are so prevalent in the county.

Turn right and follow the path with the infant river Frome on your left. Continue all around the field until arriving at a minor road. Turn left (you have now rejoined the through route) and continue over a bridge, pass the attractive Cheyney Mill, and arrive at a T junction just before a hamlet. **(1km)**

Turn right at the junction and after 200m turn left up a private drive. This leads to the attractive little group of buildings that all belonged to Cheyney Court. There is a nice little lake with a timber pavilion and a very old 'chapel' now let as a holiday cottage. Continue up towards a larger stone building which looks like an old school house. Bear right up to a timber gate and continue up the hillside beyond on an obvious sunken track.

Continue following the right hand boundary as the path rises steadily. After 500m arrive at the top corner and cross a stile into a wood. Pass through the wood and cross another stile into broken pasture. Continue following the right hand boundary to reach another stile. **(2km)**

Follow the left boundary in the next field and continue up to a further hidden stile in the top corner. Cross this and climb up the bank ahead following the left hand boundary and arrive at the top alongside a hop growing enclosure. Pass this still keeping alongside the left hand boundary, and as the path starts dropping slightly, bear right across the field to a stile in the opposite hedge. Continue across the next narrow field to another (obscured) stile and bear left in the next field to the left of buildings where find a hidden stile. Cross this and make your way along the narrow enclosed path to the main road. **(3km)** (Please note that the enclosed path can get very overgrown and there is a way through to the main road to the right of the house although this is not an official route).

Turn left and follow the pavement for 500m, past a church on the left, to reach The Wheatsheaf Inn. Cross the road and take the road alongside the pub SP Bosbury. Follow this for another 500m (lovely views towards The Malverns and also to the west) and turn off left SP Woodcroft Farm. **(4km)**

Turn off left just before the farm and continue through two sets of gates and then follow the left hand boundary through two more gates, and several (awkward) stiles towards woodland in the distance. After the second stile bear right and descend around a sunken area to find a footbridge in the hedge below. **(5km)**

Cross the bridge and ascend the bank, to reach a wide crossing track and then continue steeply uphill towards the woodland, where find a stile about 100m to the right of the left hand boundary. Pass through the wood, which can be very muddy in winter, and emerge out onto pasture. Follow the right hand boundary, but as the field widens, continue ahead and make for a stile to the left of a gate. (It is easier to unlatch the gate than to cross the stiles) Continue down the next field, bearing slightly left to pass through an avenue of oak trees and then rise up to find a stile hidden in the very top right corner of the field. **(6km)**

Walk through the wood on a narrow footpath to arrive at a broken down gate, which pass through (ignoring the footbridge on the right) to arrive in a field with crops. Continue ahead following the boundary on the right, cross a stile and then a double ended stile and footbridge **(7km)**

Continue on the same line through an open gateway, and on through a further field towards farm buildings ahead. At the next gate there is a field that can often be in crop and it may be better to follow the boundary on the right although the line is straight across the field to arrive at a gate, with steps beyond, down into the yard of Hollings Hill Farm. **(8km)**

Walk through the yard and out on to the access drive which leads up to a busy minor road. Turn left, and walk for 100m to a T junction , where turn right, SP Mathon, on to a lane. After 300m turn off left, at a footpath sign, where cross over a stile into a smallholding with a stile on the opposite side. (If there is produce growing it may be advisable to walk around the edge) Cross the access drive to another stile and follow the left hand boundary in the next field around a corner and across to a stile on the far side about 50 metres to the left of a small barn. **(9km)**

Cross the stile and follow the boundary hedge, with an orchard on your left, to arrive at another stile which cross and arrive on a lane. Take the footpath almost opposite and walk across the next long field with red brick buildings in the distance which is the village of Mathon. Make for a stile to the right of the buildings in the hedge, and then in the next field, continue ahead to find a gate on the left, with a further gate beyond, and a minor road with the church beyond. **(10km)** The Church of St John Baptist is a lovely place to stop for either a late coffee break or an early lunch stop. The church dates back to early Norman times (the tower is typical) but is regrettably mostly locked. at most times. The Yew tree in front of the entrance is an amazing example and could be up to 500 years old. There are also rather nice toilets to the rear of the church.

Leave the churchyard by the same lych gate and walk down the road towards the village. Take a footpath on the left (SP Cradley ¾ mile) just beyond a manicured yew hedge, and pass along the enclosed path to a large footbridge. Arrive at a path junction and take the right fork which is a tarmac access drive. This leads steadily uphill until just before a gate to a house, turn off to the right, up a bank to a stile, and then across a field to a further stile.

Arrive on a double track with a small quarry in front and turn left. **(11km)** Continue along the track for 500m until just before way marking signs, bear right on a fainter track . Your destination Cockshot Hill is directly up to the right but the route is initially towards a large oak tree with way marking signs visible. Before the tree it is possible to cut the corner by bearing right uphill to the woodland. Reach the fence and then follow the boundary fence up to stile at the top.

Continue on a track through the wood for 100m and reach a wide vehicular track where turn left. Follow this uphill for 200m and then along it as it levels out and follows the edge of woodland above a very attractive grassy valley. **(12km)**

Continue through two gateways, as the track drops down and then levels out as it approaches Banks Farm. Continue on the now tarmac lane, past a nicely converted house on the right, and drop down into a valley. Continue up the other side but after 100m turn off left and cross a stile into woodland. **(13km)**

After 50m bear left, and start climbing the grassy hillside on a diagonal line to a marker post above. Continue on up to a track by thorn bushes, turn right and continue to another marker post. At this post, turn half left and continue up to a metal gate. Pass through this, and another gate, and drop down to Croft Farm. Pass between the farm buildings to join an access track and continue on to reach a minor road. Turn left and follow the pavement up to a larger road. Cross this and continue up ahead on a lane past The Sugerloaf Cafe at The Elim Centre, which is a good spot to stop with refreshments and lots of goodies for sale. Walkers may well decide that a little extra sustenance is required before the last (considerable) climb of the day. **(14km)**

PLEASE NOTE that you are now entering the area of The Malvern Hills that is administered by The Conservators of The Malvern Hills. They undoubtedly do an excellent job of keeping the whole area of the hills in as natural state as possible but the downside from our point of view is that they will not allow any new way marking signs to be fixed. We have managed to put a few self adhesive signs on existing public signs but otherwise they are very limited. This situation continues on into the next stage 5 and until the main Malvern to Ledbury road is reached at Malvern Wells.

Continue climbing up the lane to arrive at a track where turn left. After 50m turn right onto a narrower track which ascends up through young trees and through a series of zigzags to arrive at plateau and a junction of paths.

This is decision time. For those ambitious walkers who are wishing to walk the through route in the quickest and shortest distance, and not wishing to stopover in Malvern, the route is to the right and on a direct hill top path to the Worcestershire Beacon, which is visible about a kilometre distant.

For those walkers finishing this stage in Malvern, there are three more possible routes. The easiest and shortest is on the wide track circling North Hill (ahead and down to the left) and known as Lady Howard de Walden Drive. The other two tracks, up North Hill, are either the contouring path which bypasses the summit or the one that goes directly to the summit. All three paths are clearly visible on a good day, but whichever route is to be taken, walkers need to initially drop down to the start of Lady Howard's track. The path to the summit is actually not too arduous and walkers should be up on top admiring all the great views within 15 minutes of leaving the plateau. The path off the summit is not well defined but is NE direction with the northerly environs of Malvern soon visible far below. The descent is very steep and care is needed. After 500m arrive at Lady Howard's track which has circumvented North Hill.

Turn right and walk along the track for 300m and reach a junction where turn sharp left SP Great Malvern, **(15km)** which is the point that walkers avoiding the summit ascent will also reach. Continue on the track which is now rather confusingly heading away from Malvern but soon turn back at a sharp bend and descend gradually to meet another wide track.

Continue ahead on the new track, past an outcrop of rock, around a deep recess in the hillside corner, and then take an earthy track which forks off to the left. Arrive at a three way junction of tracks and take the middle one which continues to descend. Roofs of houses are now visible on the left as the path continues alongside a stone wall to arrive at a track where turn left down to a minor road which is called Happy Valley.

Turn left and walk down to the town centre where there is a profusion of good pubs and cafes available for hungry and thirsty walkers. **(16km -10 miles)**

THE MALVERNS

This description is the one best known to walkers, as encompassing all the hillwalking, and with over ten named hills of over a thousand feet, it has the largest collection of high hills in Southern England.

However it could also refer to the town and all its associated outlying areas such as West Malvern, Malvern Wells etc. The inner core of Malvern is actually known as Great Malvern, which is slightly confusing, but not many people call it by that name!

Malvern, is of course, a Spa town, with many springs coming off the hillside and from which the famous waters gave the town it's importance in the 18th and 19th century. There have been many famous visitors who have come to 'take the waters' and rather like my home town of Cheltenham, it has quite a musical background, whereby it has therefore attracted composers of classical music, so that Sir Edward Elgar, who lived in the vicinity, got some of his inspiration from walking on the hills.

Due to the hilly terrain, the town has had limited expansion so that it is still a relaxing and enjoyable place to visit or stay with good transport connections. It has all modern facilities, including a very good information centre at the top of the town, where helpful staff can answer all queries from visitors.

Where 'sheep may safely graze' North Hill towards the Worcestershire Beacon

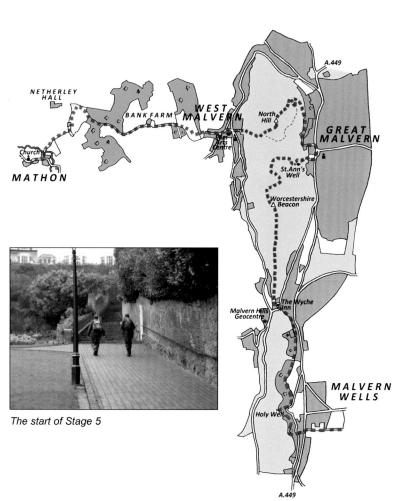

NETHERLEY HALL

BANK FARM

WEST MALVERN

Arts Centre

North Hill △

A.449

GREAT MALVERN

Church

MATHON

St. Ann's Well

Worcestershire △ Beacon

Malvern Hills Geocentre

The Wyche Inn

MALVERN WELLS

Holy Well

A.449

The start of Stage 5

North Hill △

Lady Howard De Walden Drive

Tourist Information

Priory Church

Gateway Museum

St. Ann's Well

Worcestershire △ Beacon

DETAIL AT MALVERN

A giant redwood tree near Malvern Wells

THE WYCHE WAY

STAGE 5 – Great Malvern to Upton upon Severn
(OS Explorer map 190)
17km (10.63m) Allow 4-5 hours without stops

After an initial stiff climb up to The Worcestershire Beacon, the route along the ridge is quite easygoing and thereafter is downhill all the way, with a possible stop in the attractive village of Hanley Castle at it's idiosyncratic pub.
NOTE: In the event of heavy rain in the previous week(s) walkers should check beforehand if the River Severn has burst its banks around Upton since the riverside section may be impassable and the alternative route mentioned may be necessary. This can happen once or twice a year.

Start from outside the Tourist Information Centre and cross the road to a Worcestershire Way sign where climb up steps to the road above. Cross the road, turn left on the pavement, and just after the Mount Pleasant Hotel turn right through ornamental gates into Rosebank Gardens. Follow the right hand boundary up to a large steep flight of steps where bear right at the top and arrive at a minor road. Take the track way on the opposite side and continue up the hill with signs towards St Anne's Well Café which is reached after a series of bends. It may well be too early to stop for refreshments at this excellent facility so otherwise climb the steps to the right of the building, reach a footpath and turn right. This contours around the hillside to soon reach another junction where turn left SP The Beacon, and follow this straight up the hillside, past another track on the left, to continue uphill. **(1km)**

Reach another junction at the top of the incline where turn left SP The Beacon. Follow the track around the hillside to reach a topograph with the beacon visible up on the skyline. There are a number of possibilities here but the easiest is to initially follow tracks upwards to reach a larger track which continues upwards, quite gently, but to the right of the summit. This gives good views over to the west towards Wales but soon comes up below the summit topograph which is just a little short climb up to the left. **(2kms)**

Walk over to the trig point which is just a few metres along the ridge and enjoy the great views all around from this, the highest point of the Malverns. The route from here along to The Wyche can be mostly enjoyed all along the actual top of the ridge but after 500 metres there is a lower path on the right that avoids the climb to the next summit (unnamed). Continue on the obvious paths **(3kms)** with a road now on the right which can be followed to The Wyche or continue to 'duck and dive' along the narrow paths through gorse bushes. Housing now comes into view and at this stage drop down right to

41

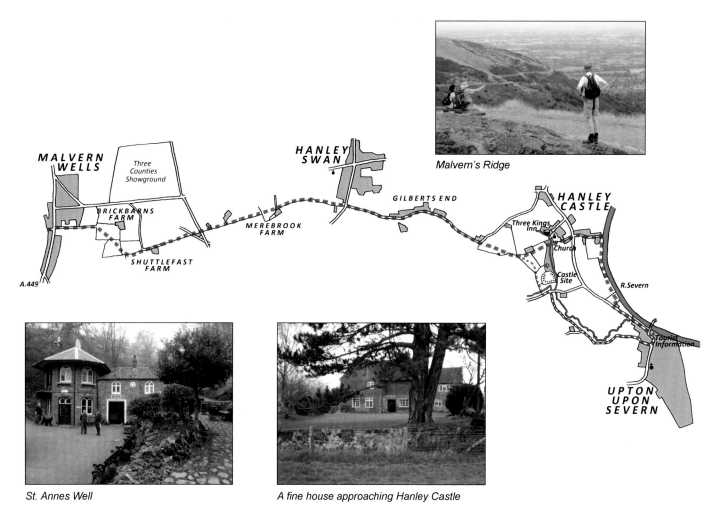

MALVERN WELLS

Three Counties Showground

BRICKBARNS FARM

SHUTTLEFAST FARM

A.449

MEREBROOK FARM

HANLEY SWAN

GILBERTS END

HANLEY CASTLE

Three Kings Inn

Church

Castle Site

R.Severn

Tourist Information

UPTON UPON SEVERN

Malvern's Ridge

St. Annes Well

A fine house approaching Hanley Castle

42

the road (if not already on it) and walk on to The Wyche. **(4kms)** where there is a large ornate bus shelter on the opposite side of the road, with an unusual Witch weathervane on the top.

Before turning left to pass through The Wyche Cutting it is worth mentioning The Malvern Hills Geocentre, which houses The Wyche Innovative Centre, and its collection of small high tech businesses. This is 100m down to the right towards Colwell. It has a really interesting information centre for all the geological strata on The Malverns and has a very good modern café.

Malvern Hills GeoCentre

Featuring Café H₂O

Information, refreshments & free wi-fi near the Wyche Cutting

www.geocentre.co.uk

THE GEOPARK WAY

This is another new linear long distance trail, that follows all the outstanding geological strata down from Bridgnorth in Shropshire to Gloucester. The 109 mile route passes through the lovely Severnside towns of Bewdley and Stourport and then crosses the river Teme to arrive on the main Malvern ridge. It drops down to Ledbury before continuing into Gloucestershire and finishing up alongside the River Severn to Gloucester.

Pass through The Wyche Cutting, and at the bend, with the aptly named and welcoming Wyche Inn on the left, turn right onto an attractive contouring track. After about 700m arrive at a junction but continue ahead on the same wide track, dropping slightly, to arrive at another junction **(5km)** where still continue ahead.
At the next junction the route continues ahead on the higher level (not down) and then soon drop down to The Holy Well which has recently been renovated and even has a bottling plant for the natural water, although there is also a steady demand from locals for their water containers to be replenished.

Walk down to the road below Holy Well, turn right, and after 200m turn off right on to a footpath. This winds its way through the woods for about 300m, until just before reaching a wide track, turn sharply left and descend quite steeply towards a minor road below. There is a wrought iron gate on the opposite side but walkers have to initially turn left to descend the bank to the road and then walk back up the road. There are a couple of the original Victorian gas lighters here which have been nicely restored and of which there are over a hundred in the Malvern area.

Drop down two flights of steps past a fine redwood tree to soon reach a larger road which is the A449 Malvern to Ledbury road. **(6km)** Cross the road, turn left, and after 50 metres turn off right into an enclosed footpath. Continue ahead following the right hand boundary over a succession of stiles. Arrive at a three way junction, fork right, and make your way across to the corner opposite. Arrive at a gate and a stile opposite which cross. Continue straight ahead, on a slightly raised causeway, towards a house ahead. **(7km)**

Just before the buildings turn left and follow the hedge on your right for 50 metres to reach a stile, which cross, and then continue on the same line as previous but with the hedge now on the left. Soon join a double track and continue past the rather nice Summer Hill House. (8km) Arrive at a minor road and cross straight over on a surfaced track which has access to Hill View stables. Soon after the track becomes unsurfaced **(9km)** where due to all the horse movements it can become very muddy and awkward but after passing through two gates it becomes easier and one soon arrives at a nice little complex of cottages. **(10km)**

Continue ahead on the same line with the spire of Hanley Swan church visible in the distance and soon reach an interesting 'Ecco' lodge with a sedum roof. The path now becomes a surfaced access track which leads on to a road junction with the village of Hanley Swan to the left. **(11km)**

Cross straight over and follow the lane for two kilometres and through the hamlet of Gilbert's End with an interesting cross section of houses to admire on route. **(13km)** The road eventually swings sharp left but we leave it and walk into the field ahead. The actual ROW is across the field to the side opposite but it may be easier to follow the right hand boundary to a way marking post. At the post is the alternative route for walkers to proceed direct to Upton if there are flood warnings but they will not only miss the river section but also the attractive village of Hanley Castle with its unusual pub. Both sections are way marked.

Take the left hand direction from the marker post and walk up to the corner of the field to a metal kissing gate. Continue straight ahead following the left hand boundary with Lodge Farm coming into view with a small ha- ha boundary in front. Arrive at another old kissing gate followed by a further kissing gate which bypass and continue on towards the church. Drop down into a copse with a bridge over a stream and then ascend a flight of steps. At the top turn left and make your way up to a metal kissing gate which gives access to the churchyard. Walk around the right hand side of the church, where those wishing to visit the pub (normal licensing hours apply) should turn left and exit the churchyard on the far side with the pub just beyond. For those, not thirsty, or at the wrong time of day, turn right beyond the church. **(14km)**

Exit the churchyard by another metal kissing gate onto Bowling Green Lane with a large modern school on the left. Follow this out to a main road where cross over carefully into Quay Lane and walk past various buildings of some antiquity to arrive adjacent to the river. Turn right and follow the well worn route **(15km)** until the path turns away from the river and proceed up to the main road. Turn left, cross to the pavement on the other side of the road and follow this into Upton upon Severn. **(16km)**

The onward route (probably for the following day) is to the left, over the fine river bridge, but those stopping in Upton, or arranging transport, should continue right into the centre where our distance is calculated to outside The White Lion Hotel, where we have often enjoyed a good tea quite often late in the day. Just before the hotel is also The Map Shop, which has probably the most comprehensive range of maps (outside London) from all around the world **(17km =10.63miles)**

The Alternative route (avoiding floods)

From the waymarking post mentioned previously, follow the right hand boundary to the corner of the field. Cross into the next field and follow the boundary in the same direction. On your left are the faint remains of Upton Castle but continue past two more field boundaries to reach a lane. Turn left but after 100m turn right and follow the lane for over a kilometre into the back of Upton. Arrive at the High Street with The White Lion Hotel on the opposite side. The distance on the alternative route is similar to the main route.

UPTON UPON SEVERN

This compact and interesting little town undoubtedly owes it's existence to the proximity of the bridge over the river. For nearly all the centuries past this was the only crossing between Worcester and Gloucester and it is well documented that in the civil war the parliamentarians advance party had a struggle to cross the rickety and damaged wooden bridge. There are still some fine old timbered buildings dating back to that time and the town has a interesting collection of small independent businesses as well as a good hotel and quite a few pubs. Rather like it's neighbouring larger towns it has maintained musical traditions and is well known for it's annual Jazz festival and several other events.

Crossing the Avon near Strensham

A.38

R.Severn

Tourist
Information

RYALL

UPTON
UPON
SEVERN

NAUNTON

M.5

UPPER
STRENSHAM

R. Avon

Strensham
Marina

ECKINGTON

Church

Railway

46

THE WYCHE WAY

STAGE 6 – Upton on Severn to Ashton under Hill
(OS Explorer map 190)
21.5km (13.44m) 6 hours walking (without stops)

This is a bit of a 'Jekyl and Hyde' day in that the morning through to a lunch stop at Eckington, is quite flat through pastoral countryside, with the focal point being the crossing of the river Avon at Strensham Lock. The afternoon provides the longest climb of the whole walk up to Parson's Folly, sitting on top of Bredon Hill, and thereafter there is an equally long descent down to Ashton under Hill.

Start from outside The White Lion Hotel and walk away from the town centre towards the river. Turn the corner, passing the tower of the old original church of St Paul, with the Tourist Information Centre inside. Turn right to cross the fine bridge over the river, and then soon turn right again onto a footpath SP Severn Way.After 100m turn left away from the river but then almost immediately turn right into an access lane to houses. This soon becomes a path which leads up to a modern curved bridge over an inlet to Upton Marina. Continue over and onto a grassy track with the houses of Ryall now visible up ahead. **(1km)**

Pass through a metal kissing gate and ascend up the enclosed path towards housing. Arrive at the corner of wooden fencing and pass through to an estate road where turn left, walk for 200m to a parking area, where turn right at a FP sign and pass between the houses. Continue through a wooden kissing gate to reach another road where continue straight across and to the right of Ryall Cottage. **(2km)**

Pass through a nice little plantation of young trees to find a stile in the top left corner which gives access to a rough paddock with another stile on the far side. Cross this and then turn right to follow the hedge through two fields with farm buildings ahead. Pass through another gate by the buildings and continue ahead on a hard track. After about 200m turn off left to cross a double stile in the hedge. Walk ahead over the broken ground to another stile. **(3km)** The route is straight ahead to another stile in the hedge opposite (200m distant) but in the event of the grass being very long or wet, it is also possible to walk on the parallel access road alongside although this is not a right of way.

Arrive at the stile in the hedge, which is not visible until the last minute since there is an earth bank obscuring it, and cross the busy main road (carefully) to reach another stile. Continue ahead in the next field following the boundary hedge on the right and then in the next field turn half right and walk across to the far corner to a finger past. Turn sharp left in the next field and follow the left hand boundary with Bredon Hill very clear up ahead in the far distance.

In the next field continue ahead, right of centre, towards housing and arrive at a trackway which leads up to a minor road and the village of Naunton. **(4km)**

Turn right, walk for 100 m, then turn left into Green Lane and proceed up to a bend with a stile and stiles opposite. Cross over and continue across the field with a nice black and white timbered farmhouse on the right. Make for a double metal gate opposite and then in the next field follow the right hand boundary hedge up to the top right corner where pass through a gate on the right and then follow the left hand boundary up towards a ridge ahead. Cross over a small bridge and a stile and continue up ahead to the top of the ridge. **(5km)**

Cross a stile on the right into the next field, but immediately after, climb steps up to another stile on the left into another field. The route ahead is slightly right of centre but initially it is probably best to follow the left hand boundary up and over the crest of the hill, where we can see the village of Upper Strensham ahead. It is then possible to see a stile down on the opposite side of the field, about 200m out from the left hand corner.

Cross the stile and a crossing track and continue over another stile and head towards a band of woodland.

Continue on to the left of the woodland with a pond also on the left. **(6km)** The path then becomes enclosed and is quite narrow in places as we ascend up to the top and arrive on a surfaced track and then onto a road, passing attractive buildings on both sides. Shortly after arrive at the centre of this attractive village with a small green, where turn right, to find a bus shelter and a wide grass verge which provides a good place to enjoy a mid morning refreshment break.

Continue out of the village and at a T junction turn left and cross the M5 motorway. **(7km)** Just after the bridge find a footpath (can be overgrown) on the left and descend down a flight of steps to a large field. Turn left and follow the boundary of the field. (parallel to the motorway) The actual footpath goes diagonally across this large field but when the crops are high I have found it better to continue parallel to the motorway for about 300m and then to join a wide vehicular track which then leads across the field for about 500m to a band of woodland ahead. **(8km)**

At the end of the track, and just by the woodland, turn left for 10m, and then right. The route is diagonally across the field past two electricity poles but since the field is often in crop it is usually better to circle around the right hand boundary. The stile into the woodland is difficult to locate and the author may well have to do some severe pruning around it to aid visibility!

Cross the stile and drop steeply down steps and along the slippery path that leads through the scrubby woodland (at the time of writing this there was an interesting wicker sculpture in the wood) to a double stile and an access lane. Turn right for about 100m and then left on to another access road to Strensham Lock and it's old mill. **(9km)** This is a major mooring centre on the River Avon and has been tastefully developed. Pass through either of the entrance gates and bear right past a stag sculpture to the left of the old mill. Pass under some wooden beams and then turn left through a doorway to arrive at a metalled walkway over the sluice stream. Continue alongside the river to arrive at another, even more impressive, metal walkway over another sluice. After about 200m arrive at a lock, and cross the bridge to emerge onto the aptly named, Mill lane.

Continue up the lane which ascends gently up towards the village of Eckington **(10km)** Arrive at a road junction and continue straight ahead up to a high stepped bridge over the railway with the commodious Bell Inn alongside the major road. After hopefully a good lunch stop, cross the road carefully and walk up Cotheridge Lane opposite. Pass The Anchor Inn and soon after, turn left at the next junction, and then right into School Lane SP Village Hall. This leads steadily up hill but just before the top, turn right into Stony Furlong Lane with a gate into open pasture beyond. **(11km)** Continue through two fields on the obvious path and then in the next large field bear half left on a line for prominent buildings in the distance. The path drops down into a dip with two stiles in wire fencing and then continues on the same line up to a gate with a road beyond. **(12km)**

Turn left and after about 300m turn off right into another large field. Continue up this field to emerge onto the private driveway of St Catherine's Farm. **(13km)** Continue up past the house and onto a gravelled drive that leads to Woollas Hall, a fine old house, with a number of ancillary cottages. Just after the house spot a stile with a Wychavon Way sign **(14km)** (to be followed all the way to Ashton under Hill) and climb up the hillside to soon arrive at another stile, with a stony path beyond. Turn right and follow this up the hill to a fork, where turn right again, and then very soon after bear left up the hill following a line of posts.

After about 500 m arrive a gateway which continue through and up a gully. Arrive at another gate on the edge of woodland, **(15km)** pass through, turn left onto a broad track and continue upwards with great views over to the left, to arrive at Parsons Folly.

PARSONS FOLLY

This was possibly built in the late 18th century, for William Parsons, who was the squire of Kemerton village, which lies to the south of Bredon Hill. It makes a great landmark from afar and was built so that the top of

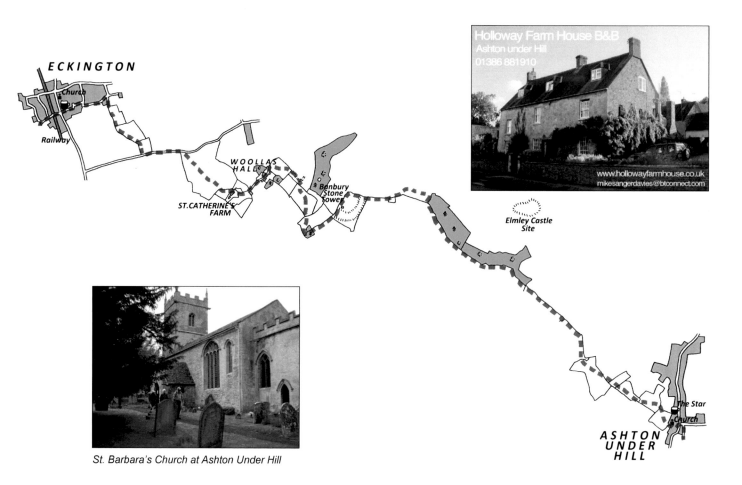

ECKINGTON

Church

Railway

WOOLLAS HALL

ST. CATHERINE'S FARM

Banbury Stone Tower

Holloway Farm House B&B
Ashton under Hill
01386 881910

www.hollowayfarmhouse.co.uk
mikesangerdavies@btconnect.com

Elmley Castle Site

The Star
Church

ASHTON UNDER HILL

St. Barbara's Church at Ashton Under Hill

the tower was 1000 feet above sea level. This was not an unusual occurrence in that Broadway Tower which marks the end of our walk has the same distinction, as does Alfred's Tower at Stourhead in Wiltshire, and also the tower on Leith Hill in Surrey. This tower is now used as a mobile phone base station.

Continue along the escarpment from the tower which initially means walking away from the wall and around a big hollow with distinctive stones lying on the bottom. Arrive back near the wall and follow the lovely grassy track heading for a clump of scots pines in the distance. Ignore a path off to the left and carry on ahead to a gate alongside the pines. **(16km)** Soon after take a right fork and follow the fence line to a metal gate and a band of woodland. Pass through the gate and follow the path with the woodland on your left hand side. **(17km)** Continue on the same line, pass another footpath on the right, to arrive at an ornamental wooden bench commemorating The Wychavon Way. **(18km)** Continue on the same line to pass through an open gateway with views now opening up ahead to the Cotswold Hills.

The path now starts descending **(19km)** and at the end of a field the path bears right for 50m to a gate which pass through and descend more steeply **(20km)** to arrive at a fork where take the right path. Arrive at a metal gate and pass through the separate pedestrian gate and continue on down now following a hedge on the left. After 300m cross a stile into the next field with views of Ashton under Hill below and continue on a diagonal line to a further stile. Continue to a waymarking post through a copse of trees and into open pasture, following Wychavon Way signs past a further stile, and with a boundary fence about 100 m over to the right. **(21km).** The village church is now in view but make for the right hand of two waymarks in the fence below.

Cross a stile onto a track and then pass down over steps to an old stone stile to arrive in pasture, where bear slightly right and make for the right of the churchyard. Continue along the side of the churchyard through two wooden kissing gates to arrive alongside the attractive St Barbara's Church with a lyche gate and the road beyond. **(21.6km= 13.5m)**

ASHTON UNDER HILL
Ashton is quite a long village and definitely an active one. Population is about 800 but it has a large school that attracts parents from surrounding villages. The attractive Star Inn remains busy with a good range of food and drinks and there are a few bed and breakfast opportunities in the village. There is a good village shop at the northern end. The village runs a very successful Open Gardens weekend in June which raises considerable funds towards local causes. There is also a good bus service (No 540) which runs between Cheltenham, Tewkesbury and Evesham.

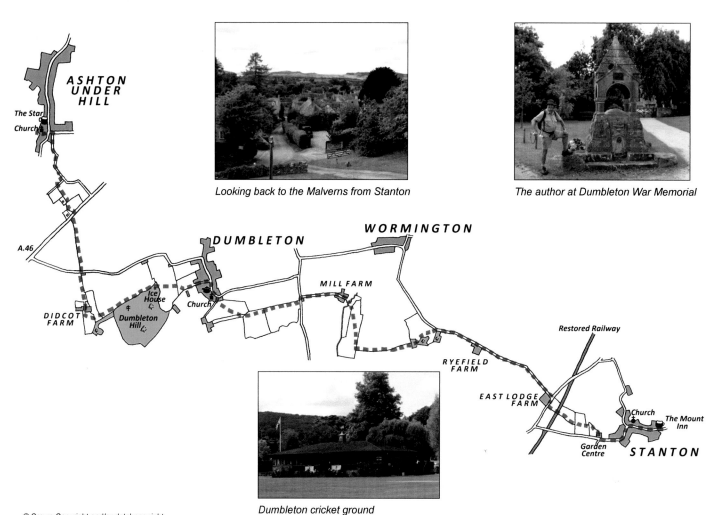

ASHTON UNDER HILL

The Star

Church

A.46

DIDCOT FARM

Ice House

Dumbleton Hill

DUMBLETON

Church

Looking back to the Malverns from Stanton

The author at Dumbleton War Memorial

WORMINGTON

MILL FARM

Dumbleton cricket ground

RYEFIELD FARM

EAST LODGE FARM

Restored Railway

Garden Centre

Church

The Mount Inn

STANTON

THE WYCHE WAY

STAGE 7 – Ashton under Hill to Broadway Tower
OS Explorer map(s) 190 & OL45
18km (11.25m) Allow 4 - 5 hours without stops

This is a day of two halves. The morning is through the Vale of Evesham with a possible refreshment stop in the lovely village of Dumbleton, before continuing across to the classical village of Stanton and the welcoming Mount Inn. The afternoon route is then up onto the Cotswold escarpment, where we pass through Snowshill, and finish up at the Tower.

Start from outside The Star Inn, and walk down to the road junction where turn left SP Evesham, and almost immediately turn right again into a lane SP Rails End Nursery. Continue straight on at the next junction which is now SP The Wychavon Way. After 500m the lane rises slightly to cross a former railway line, but bear right and cross a footbridge. Shortly after turn right and follow the path alongside a hedge with an open field to the right.

After 200m, turn left off the path through a pedestrian gate, and walk up alongside an avenue of poplar trees towards buildings ahead. **(1km)** Walk around the corner of a bungalow and join an access road which leads up towards the main road. After 100 metres the road bears left but we continue straight ahead on an enclosed footpath that leads up to the busy A 435. Turn right and walk for 100m towards a blind bend and cross very carefully to a bridle way on the opposite side. This straight track is now on a kind of causeway which leads up to a minor road. Continue on the other side which is a driveway to Didcot Farm. **(2km)** Arrive at the farmyard and initially bear right but then left to pass through two pairs of metal gates. Turn left to walk across the pasture and through another metal gate. The direction is then towards a footbridge in the far hedge, but beware of the ground in between, which can be extremely boggy and where it may be advisable to detour around on either side.

Cross the footbridge and bear right up towards the woodland to find a pedestrian gate. **(3km)** Turn left on the path which winds its way along the edge of the wood (bluebells in the spring) for about 500m, before exiting the woodland onto pasture with great views over to Ashton under Hill with Bredon Hill beyond. Continue high in the field until another pedestrian gate is reached for access into more woodland. Immediately you will see on your right a bricked entrance to a kind of cave in the bank. This was originally a Ice House for the nearby Dumbleton Hall, which is now a hotel with all modern conveniences, including refrigeration!

Leave the woodland and follow the footpath down through the parkland to another gate with views ahead of Dumbleton, Bear right in the next field to find a stile in metal fencing with an access track on the other side. Turn left and walk down towards houses, but not before admiring the lovely cricket ground, which is one of the finest village grounds in Gloucestershire.

The track now leads into Dairy Lane which has some fine houses on either side and which then meets the main village street. Turn right and walk along to the war memorial outside the church, but do also call in at the village stores, now rather more of a cafe, with all sorts of goodies available. **(4km)**

Continue up the road to a T junction with the entrance to Dumbleton Hall hotel on the right. Cross the road to a stile opposite, where in the large field beyond there are two footpaths. Take the left fork which initially follows the hedge on the left but then proceeds straight across the field to a gap in the far hedgerow.

Pass through the gap and turn sharp left onto a double trackway. Follow the hedge on the left for 500m to a minor road. **(5km)** You will have clear views of Broadway Tower on the skyline which looks nearer than it is! Turn left on the road, and then almost immediately turn right for Mill Farm. Proceed up this manicured drive but just before the house bear left and walk between the farm buildings. You will soon see a large pedestrian bridge, ahead and down below, which after crossing, turn right

and follow the rough grassy tracks for 200m to another smaller bridge on your left. The ruined mill from which the farm takes its name can be seen with the remnants of a wheel over on the right. **(6km)**

Cross the second bridge, and pass through a gate soon after. Make your way straight across the field to the hedgerow opposite and turn right around the corner to find another footpath joining from the left. Turn right and follow the hedge for about 500m to reach an opening on the left which pass through and now follow the hedge on the right as the path rises up steadily. **(7km)**

Arrive at the corner of the field, turn right through an opening and then left to follow another hedge on the left. Proceed ahead towards woodland but just before the corner bear right slightly to gain access into the wood on a wide and muddy vehicular trackway. Follow the track through the wood and out into pasture on the other side. After about 100m fork left off the trackway and make your way across to a metalled gate with a minor road beyond.

Follow this quiet road (**8km** halfway along) for about 1.5km until a main road is reached (B4632 Winchcombe to Broadway) **(9km)**. Turn right and walk carefully along the road for 100m to find a broken down footpath sign on the opposite side. Cross the narrow field to a stile and a footbridge over the newly restored track of the

Cheltenham to Broadway railway. A very unusual feature of this bridge, which the author has never seen before, is the provision of a separate water channel under the bridge to take flood water from one side to the other.

The Cheltenham to Stratford Railway

Known as The Honeybourne line, this double track railway was built between 1900 and 1906. It survived the Beeching cuts in the 1960's but was closed after damage to the track bed in 1976. However it has been partially restored by volunteers since 1984 with steam trains running on a regular basis. It should be restored from Cheltenham Racecourse to Broadway by 2018 which will represent about two thirds of the original length.

Pass through a gate on the other side of the bridge and continue ahead with a hedge on the right up to a rather decrepit old barn. **(10km)** Walk around the back and then pass through a gate on the left and continue on the same line as before with a hedge on the left and a band of woodland ahead. Continue past a rather larger and more attractive barn on the left, to a gate where pass through, and bear right across the next field. Make your way to the left of agricultural buildings, which are all part of a rather interesting plant and garden centre.

Pass alongside an unusual piece of topiary and arrive at a side gate, alongside a main gate, with a minor road beyond. Turn left and continue up the road into the lovely village of Stanton. This must be one of the most quintessential Cotswold villages for admirers to appreciate, and there are many very old and beautiful houses alongside as we walk up to a junction. You may notice that the stone used on the houses is not quite as pale as other Cotswold stone, and this is since there is some orange coloured ironstone, which is more typical of the Stratford upon Avon area, and which is only about ten miles further north. Continue straight ahead up the main street, and after passing a turning off to the right, our route starts climbing and soon the welcoming Mount Inn is seen up ahead. **(11km)**

The Donnington Brewery

The Mount Inn is one of seventeen pubs owned by this Cotswold brewery, which is based near Stow on the Wold, at the attractive village of the same name. It is set in beautiful surroundings, which include it's own mill pond. The brewery will be celebrating its 150th anniversary this year with just the 4th generation of the Arkell family at the helm. The business has always been very family based, in that publicans and staff, have always been regarded much as family members.

Leave from the front door of the pub and walk across the driveway to a stepped path which leads up the hillside. Pass through a gate where the path now becomes unsurfaced and continues upwards in a series of bends

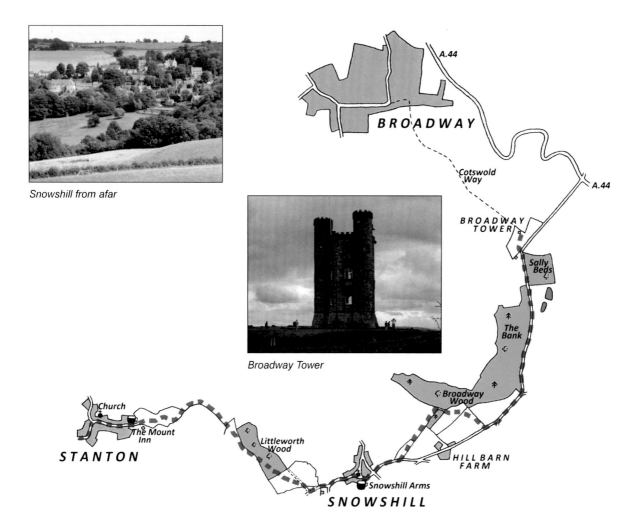

Snowshill from afar

Broadway Tower

STANTON

Church
The Mount Inn

Littleworth Wood

Snowshill Arms

SNOWSHILL

Broadway Wood

HILL BARN FARM

The Bank

Sally Beds

BROADWAY TOWER

Cotswold Way

BROADWAY

A.44

56

until eventually it levels out. **(12km)** Pass through another gate and then arrive at a kind of plateau with a major path crossing which is The Cotswold Way. Continue straight ahead, now on a road for about 500m, until soon after, when the road starts dropping, turn off left onto a narrow path through Littleworth Wood.

Follow the waymarked path for about 400m, until emerging out onto sloping pasture, with a lovely view of Snowshill village across the valley. **(13km)** Continue on a diagonal line down to a gate in the far corner and emerge on to a track. Turn right to reach a lane, where turn left, and walk past spacious properties to reach another road junction. Turn left and walk down into this lovely village, where just before reaching the Snowshill Arms, (another good Donnington pub) turn off right into the churchyard, and walk up to the war memorial, which is a good spot to admire the village and maybe have a short afternoon break.

Walk out of the churchyard onto a lane and continue up the hill, past more interesting properties, to arrive at a T junction. **(14km)** Cross over and continue on up the hill SP Broadway Tower. After about 400m turn off left at a stile and continue along the top of the field close to a wall on the right but with fine views on the left for many miles. You are now walking along the top of age old quarries and the path eventually arrives at the corner of the field with woodland opposite.

Cross a stile on the right and continue on a path, that initially climbs up a bank, but then levels out, as it continues alongside the woodland on your left. Pass through a gate **(15km)** and then shortly after, the path moves away from the woodland and crosses over the corner of the field to arrive at a further metal gate in the far corner. Follow the enclosed footpath to a further gate and then pass alongside a sizeable sawmill to reach a minor road. Very regrettably the route from here to Broadway Tower is nearly all on minor roads but there is little traffic. Turn left, walk up to junction where fork left and. continue on for another 600m to a further road junction, where fork left again SP Broadway Tower.

Continue along this narrower lane for about 1.5km to arrive at the Broadway Country Park. Initially turn off left, but do notice that there is a very good cafe just below which has a great range of refreshments. However our onward route is through a high deer proof gate, (the herd of deer are often visible within the park) where bear right, and continue for 400m to reach the tower, which is your final destination. **(17km 10.63m)**

Broadway Tower

This fine building was originally built as a folly in the late 18th century for The Earl of Coventry, whose country seat was at Earls Croome. some twenty miles distant between Upton on Severn and Pershore. The original design was probably by Capability Brown but was later built under the auspicies of James Wyatt. It was built to be visible from Croome Park and on occasions a beacon was also lit on the hill. The tower was later leased out to Sir Thomas Phillips, a noted bibliophile, who installed a printing press for the reproduction of antiquarian pamphlets. In the late 19th century it was further leased to William Morris, whose Arts and Crafts movement was active in nearby Chipping Campden. The view from the top of the tower is really inspiring, with apparently up to ten counties visible in the distance, and this together with all the pictorial information is worthy of paying the necessary fee to ascend to the top.

Although our trail officially finishes here, there are still more options, unless you have transport collecting you from the Country Park. Firstly, continue just past the tower, where in a dip, there is another deer proof gate with way marking signs. All onward routes pass through the gate, where those wishing to finish in Broadway should turn left and follow The Cotswold Way (South) for about 2km, down into the village, where there is accommodation, local buses for Evesham and a mainline train service to London and Birmingham.

Those walkers who wish to continue on to Chipping Campden, and even to continue on down to London by connecting up with The Shakespeare's Way *(see page 75)*, will need to continue ahead from the deer proof gate, and to follow The Cotswold Way. (North) After about 1.5km they will arrive at the very busy A44 with the large Fish Hill (free) car park opposite. This is another good point for leaving a car or for arranging collection. Please note that this car park is locked from dusk to dawn.

BROADWAY

It is rather surprising that this large village is not actually a town since it has a population of nearly 3000. It takes it's name from the wide and tree lined main street and it has been called The Jewel in The Cotswolds . The world famous Lygon Arms hotel, in the middle of the village, was at one time owned by the Russell family, and it was the son, Gordon who became a designer of fine furniture, that made his fame, with the ensuing honour of a well deserved knighthood. There is plenty of other accommodation and lots of individual shops but the village can get exceedingly busy at times.

THE WYCHE WAY

ACROSS TWO COUNTRIES

It is quite important when setting out any walking book to show an outline for the part of the country on which the walk is based. As soon as I looked at the location of The Wyche Way I realized that it lay almost exactly in the middle of a line from the Welsh coast at Aberystwyth down to London. I also knew that there were long distance trails that could easily be used to connect up from either side. With regard to these established trails, it is a very good idea to look at the details on the internet, since any changes to the route may well be shown there, whilst guide books may not have been reprinted or updated.

The route descriptions for the existing trails are already well documented and are mostly shown on the relevant OS maps so that my route observations are only general. I have shown more detailed description where there has to be a link between existing LD trails but these are only my suggested routes and are not way marked so that enterprising walkers may well have their own ideas for making their own route. Long distance walkers are often on quite a tight time schedule so that sometimes my route(s) are on quiet country lanes rather than obscure footpaths.

I had never previously thought of Aberystwyth as much of a walking destination until, a few years ago, a friend of mine in the LDWA (Long Distance Walking Association) said she was interested in doing the 'Across Wales' challenge event. This is a very demanding 45 mile walk? that starts at Anchor Bridge, which is on the border with England a few miles SE of Newtown. It finishes at Aberystwyth on the same day after a very early start and competitors are allowed just 18 hours for the route through very remote countryside which also includes the ascent of Plynlimon.

I had visions of putting this on for my own Wiltshire group of the LDWA, but over two full days. Even that was not workable with the accommodation and transport logistics, let alone what would still be a very demanding trip, so it remained on the back burner, but not out of mind.

I first went up to Aberystwyth in early 2014, just after the storms that had swept across England and Wales, and found the town badly affected with stone and shingle all over the seafront, so that it was not at all inviting. However six months later it was a great summer's day and the front was looking lovely. There is an information board that compares Aberystwyth with Brighton and certainly it is probably the best destination place in West Wales. Like Brighton, it also has a large university, which makes for a younger population, and there is no shortage of interesting pubs and restaurants in the town.

I remembered my previous interest but in the meantime I had also heard very good reports about The Wye Valley Walk which starts just below Plynlimon and which would make a far easier route down towards The Wyche Way, but first of all I had to look at a route out of Aberystwyth to get to it, which was by no means straightforward.

The summit of Plynlimon

A swinging bridge over the River Wye

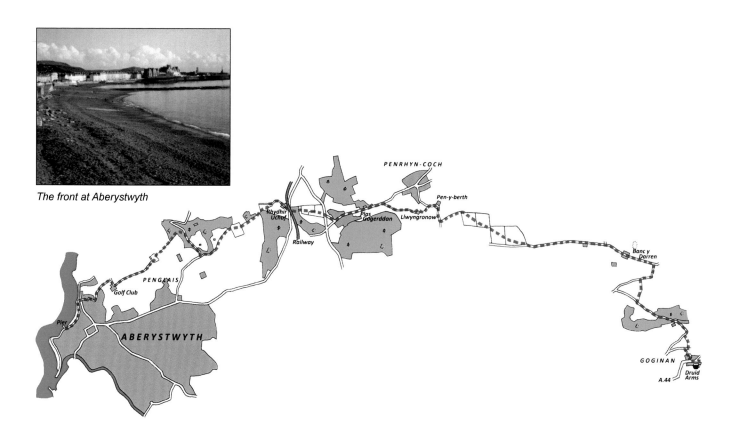

The front at Aberystwyth

PENRHYN-COCH

Pen-y-berth

Rhydhir
Uchaf

Plas
Gogerddan

Llwyngronow

Railway

Banc y
Darren

PENGLAIS

Golf Club

Pier

ABERYSTWYTH

GOGINAN

A.44

Druid
Arms

THE WELSH CONNECTION
Aberystwyth to Pont Rhydgaled (A44) via Plylimon
46km (28.75m)

You will see that I have included basic maps in the book for these connecting walks but they are based on the Landranger 1:50000 series, and as explained below, the more detailed Explorer maps are vital for good progress on the ground. Planning is most important for any long distance walk and for anyone starting out on this trip, an early purchase of the guide book for The Wye Valley Walk would be helpful, even if the route description runs south to north .The Explorer maps 213 Aberystwyth and 214 cover the first twenty miles of the WVW. The difficulty is that the WVW does not actually get to the source of the River Wye, which is high on Plynlimon, in a rather impenetrable spot, especially in mist. It is certainly possible to achieve a through route but a fall back alternative is advisable.

This is possible for those walkers, who may be short of time, nervous about Plynlimon, or doubtful about the weather, who can easily use the regular bus service that runs up and down the A44 from Llangurig to Aberystwyth.

The route for my own first day was 25.5km (16 miles) through to Ponterwyd, where there is accommodation and which is also on the A44. I found a nice quick way out

of the town through The Penglais Country Park which soon gets you high, and alongside the Aberystwyth golf course. My mid morning coffee stop was taken in the lee of buildings belonging to the University of Wales but previously a centre for environmental research. (map ref 629836) Thereafter I found a lack of footpath signs and even some stiles, so that I eventually took to a long quiet lane, with good views that led me in the rough direction of Goginan, which was my lunchtime destination. The village was clearly visible some way distant but there was still some more tricky navigation before I arrived at the rustic but welcoming Druid Arms. It had taken 5 hours to walk the 10 miles from Aberystwyth, thanks to the difficult route finding. The village is also on the A44 and the bus can stop near to the pub. (check opening hours if planning to stop.)

The afternoon started well, with an easy but quite steep climb up from the village on another quiet lane. I then found a lovely high level track that led eastwards to Pen-rhiwlas, continued on to Bwa-drain and then on to a minor road overlooking Lyn-yr-Oerfa. Still continuing eastwards, past Pant-y-ffynnon, and on a nice moorland track I realized that I should have turned off NE. However the track was still heading eastwards and eventually bought me out onto an unfenced road south west of Ponterwyd. This last bit of walking had all been on open access land so that my route was certainly legitimate! and was definitely more straightforward than

63

Approaching Llangurig

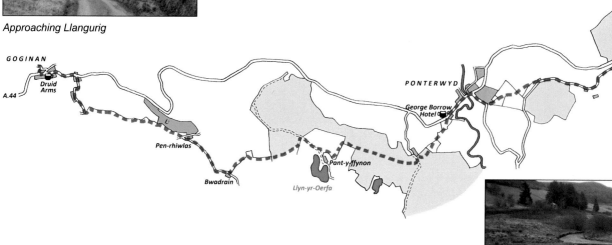

GOGINAN

A.44

Druid
Arms

Pen-rhiwlas

Bwadrain

Pant-y-ffynon

Llyn-yr-Oerfa

PONTERWYD

George Borrow
Hotel

DYFFRYN
CASTELL

A.44

The River Wye outside Llangurig

I had originally planned. I turned left on an unfenced road and was soon looking down a valley towards Ponterwyd. Just by a cattle grid I turned off the road and onto an obvious track (with an actual FP sign!) which contoured around the hillside and then dropped down into the valley with houses of the village getting nearer. The footpath conveniently comes out just below The George Borrow Hotel, named after the famous 19c traveller, and useful for accommodation. There is also a B&B just outside the village in the Aberystwyth direction.

There is not a lot to Ponterwyd, but there is a garage, which also has quite a comprehensive shop for stocking up on provisions which would be vital for the following day. The ascent of Plynlimon starts just a few miles further down the A44 at the old (now ruined) Dyffryn Castell Inn- where buses can stop if you are not overnighting in Ponterwyd. There is a further alternative to the ascent of Plynlimon, if one is not walking through to Dyffryn Castell, whereby with the bus or a car, there is a shorter ascent possible, with less climbing, from a further couple of miles down (east) the A44 at Eisteddfa Gurig. The route from here is due west through a large complex of buildings and it is then only about a mile to join the main track up from Dyffryn Castell. There is also a further more direct route to the summit which heads north from the buildings but this appears to peter out soon after a disused mine but it could be worth looking at in good visibility. Otherwise, from Ponterwyd, walkers proceed down the main road, past the garage, and just after crossing a bridge, turn right onto the A4120 Devil's Bridge road. Just up the hill and past a modern housing development turn left onto a bridle way.

The route passes through a wood and then a field to arrive at a minor road B4343. Turn left and follow this for 2 km to reach the A44 where turn right and continue to The Dyffryn Castell Inn. I can remember having a drink in this large establishment when walking The Cambrian Way in the '90s. It has been unoccupied now for well over a decade, and my guess is that the owner will eventually seek a demolition order and get planning permission for something a lot more practical , probably holiday homes.

This is now decision time in that the ascent up to the summit of Plynlimon is probably 2 hours walking. A further half an hour is then n eeded to reach the source of the River Wye and then at least another hour down (over steep rough ground) to join a spur track to the official Wye Valley Walk.

It is then about 3 miles down to the A44 (bus stop) with a further 7 miles down on the WWW to Llangurig. So overall from Ponterwyd to Llangurig would be about 20 miles taking the whole route over Plylimon, which makes for a very long day. However, as explained, this can be slightly shortened and the last few miles into

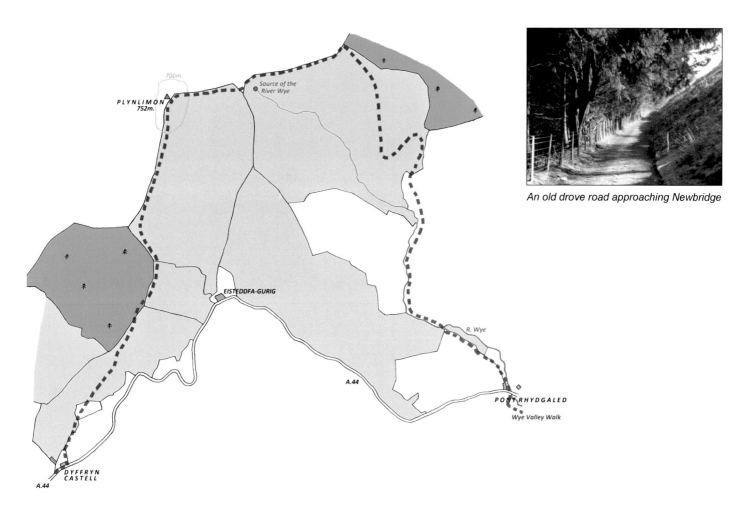

An old drove road approaching Newbridge

700m.

PLYNLIMON
752m.

Source of the
River Wye

EISTEDDFA-GURIG

R. Wye

A.44

PONT RHYDGALED

Wye Valley Walk

DYFFRYN
CASTELL

A.44

Llangurig can also be done on the main road if the light is fading. On my last recce I was actually driving out from Aberystwyth so I waited for the Tourist Information to open to get a more accurate picture on the mountain weather since it was rather gloomy in the town. They said that visibility on Plynlimon was 1000 feet for the morning rising to 1500 feet in mid afternoon. Plynlimon is actually 2500 feet high! but I still decided to go for it. In the end, visibility was certainly patchy, but this kind of forecast and weather conditions, are very much the norm for Plylimon. The mountain has sometimes been described as a sodden weariness!

The ascent from Dyffryn Castell is fairly straightforward with waymarking signs fairly evident every 500metres or so. It gets a little sketchy after a mile but there are more posts up ahead and soon woodland becomes visible on the left and the path follows this up to a large area of surfaced track. Beyond the forest, now at 600 metres height, a fence line is followed almost all the way to the summit. There is also a track which is over to the right and the two eventually meet up. The actual summit cairn is then sighted on the western side of the fence which is reached by crossing a large ladder stile. For the continuation to the source of the River Wye, it is necessary to continue on the eastern side of the fence which almost immediately bears sharp right. Follow this for nearly a kilometre past two cairns. After the second cairn, follow the fence line as it now bears south east.

After 300m another fence is reached, which should be crossed and the source of the Wye is just 200m due east, downhill, in a hollow. Map ref - SN803 871 It is certainly not very prepossessing and in dry weather not very obvious. For my ongoing route, and to be certain in the swirling mist, I initially walked back due north for about 200m to reach the fence line. I then turned right and followed it for nearly 2km until woodland was sighted ahead. I then turned south, picking out the best of the ground, and descended, but moved further away from the woodland to avoid the steeper gradients. This was now on a fairly gentle ridge which eventually led down to a grassy double track. Map ref SN821859

Turn left on the track, which contours down around the hillside, and after about a kilometre join the official Wye Valley Walk where turn right.(south) This is now a wide vehicular track which descends gradually through gates to a wide open area which is used for the Sweet Lamb Rally centre. The track continues on down to eventually meet the A44 at Pont Rhydgaled with the continuation of the WVW almost opposite on the other side of the main road.

THE WYE VALLEY WALK
Pont Rhydgaled to Builth Wells 57 km (35.5m)
Explorer maps 214 and 200.

The WVW originally finished at Rhayader but over the years it has been extended, up to and as close as it can get to the actual source. The point where it passes over the infant river at Pont Rhydgaled on the A44 is, for me, the formal start of the walk. The 7 miles down to Llangurig is very pleasant with a mixture of riverside walking, some upland walking and passes remote little farmsteads. It is well waymarked and progress can be reasonably fast with much of the route on surfaced tracks. There is no accommodation between Llangurig and Rhayader which is a further 12 miles on, so a stop in Llangurig (one of the highest villages at 300m in Wales) will mostly be necessary. Both the pubs have accommodation and there is also a large B&B nearby. In addition there is a small village shop for simple provisions. The next section to Rhayader starts with a nice easy bit of lane walking before climbing quite steeply up onto the flanks of Esgair Dernol, which at 476m (1523ft) is one of the higher points on the whole trail. The route then drops down to follow the river until after about 8 miles from Llangurig the river is crossed on a narrow pedestrian bridge and the A44 is reached..

The official route here has now been changed and follows the vehicular route to Gilfach where there is a visitor centre (not often open) and also a nice stone bothy in the buildings, which makes for a good dry picnic stop. The route then turns due south, crosses a high ridge before joining a lane for the last couple of miles into Rhayader. (Note - the road walking on the WVW is quite a high percentage. I would estimate it as maybe 20% of the total)

Rhayader is a busy little town of 2000 population, which is set on a crossroads of two major roads the A44 and the A470. It is also the gateway to the huge Elan reservoirs which attract many visitors. The town has plenty of accommodation, lots of pubs and a good range of different shops. It is also the terminus for long distance buses from South Wales and the Midlands.

The next stage of the WVW is rather longer at 26.5km (16.5m) but the large village of Newbridge on Wye (just off the route) lies just over halfway with both a pub and a shop handy for refreshments. The route out of Rhayader is quite similiar to the previous stage in that there is an immediate climb up to 395m (1300ft) before dropping down to the attractive village of Llanwrthwl and then following quite close to the river to Newbridge. Thereafter the river is still kept in close proximity all the way to Builth.

The unfrequented hills towards Hundred House

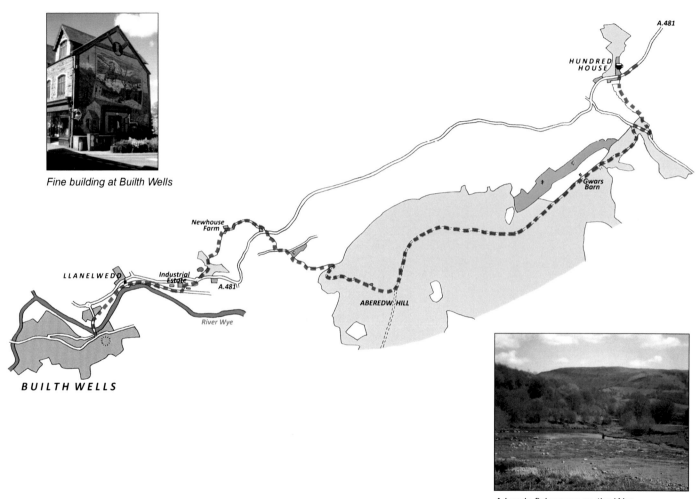

Fine building at Builth Wells

A.481

HUNDRED HOUSE

Gwars Barn

Newhouse Farm

LLANELWEDD

Industrial Estate

A.481

River Wye

ABEREDW HILL

BUILTH WELLS

A lonely fisherman on the Wye

Builth Wells is a little larger than Rhayader and rather more spacious. It is home to the very successful Royal Welsh show every July when accommodation is booked for miles around but otherwise there are plenty of services in this attractive town.

BUILTH WELLS to KINGTON 33km (20.5m)

There are two options for this last bit of walking in Wales and for reaching The Wyche Way. The most direct route is due east from Builth across the unfrequented hills that lie north of Hay on Wye. There is little convenient accommodation before Gladestry which is reached at 25.5km (16m) although I have taken my route via Hundred House where there is a pub of the same name which also has accommodation.. There are two camp sites, one just before Hundred House and the other one high on a bank behind the pub. This is one of the remotest parts of Mid Wales with rolling hills, interesting hamlets, and a fascinating little church at Colva. This was an area much visited by the Reverend Kilvert and mentioned in his famous diaries.

After the good waymarking on the WWW it was a bit of a shock to revert to the previous 'hunt the route' experienced out of Aberystwyth. However the route out of Builth started well enough on an old railway line (now National Cycle path 8) which led after a mile, to an industrial estate with an exit to the A470. Just over the road is an unsigned track which leads steeply up hillside and passes through gates to arrive at Newhouse Farm where there is an access lane that leads back down to the A470.

Cross the road, turn left, and within 50 metres pass through a rusty old gate. (no sign in 2014). The route goes up the left hand side of the field where find another gate with access to a positive track. Turn left and after 200m turn off right onto a waymarked bridle path. This leads up to the edge of the escarpment, where turn right and climb quite steeply up the hillside, to reach an old quarry, where turn left to arrive up on the open moorland.

Continue ahead on the obvious track on this remote but attractive moorland. I didn't take a narrow path on the left, but continued on to reach a small pond, whereafter I turned off left to reach another track after about 200m. I then turned left again and started a gentle climb making for higher ground to the North. A look at the map will show that wherever, one needs to be almost on the northern edge of the escarpment. After about a further mile I got a view of a large plantation ahead, and although I started thinking that this was the best way to get to Hundred House, I soon realized that I needed to pass the plantation and I descended past the (rather rundown) Gwars Barn to eventually arrive down at a minor road. I then turned right and walked 300m to pick up a footpath on the left which led through a series of wet fields to arrive almost opposite the pub. It is quite old

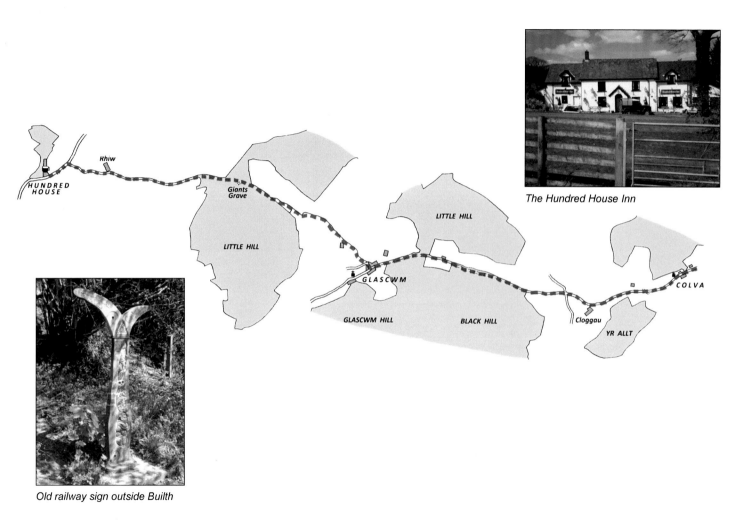

The Hundred House Inn

Old railway sign outside Builth

72

and small but the welcome was warm and refreshments reasonably priced. They also have three or four letting rooms for Bed and Breakfast. Readers will have to excuse the extra detail given on this section from Builth but the potential to take a wrong route is quite easy.

My route from Hundred House was happily more straightforward and proceeded up the main road for nearly 500m to take the second lane on the right. (No through road sign) This wound steadily uphill for about 1.5km until arriving at a gate with a rough(4 wheel drive) track beyond. This topped out at about 440m height before descending through several gates to reach a tarmac road at Glascwm. Turn left on this quiet little lane which passes between hills on either side to reach after another 5km (3 miles+)the lovely little church at Colva. There are rather thoughtful facilities here in the church for DIY tea or coffee. I then continued along the same lane for a further 1.5km to reach the large farm at Upper Gwernilla where I turned off left and passed behind the farm buildings to find (a rather obscure!) bridle path that lead through a series of fields to the hamlet of Newhouse. I then joined a footpath that took me down to the B4594 just south of Gladestry.

This latter route is all quite sketchy, with little or no waymarking, so walkers may decide it is faster and less hassle to take the parallel lane which also joins the B4594, although it is a little further south. However walkers may well be tired of hard tarmac under foot for much of the way from Hundred House? Gladestry is an attractive little village and has a rather nice pub The Royal Oak, which is very walker friendly, with four letting rooms as well as a bar with real ales, and good food. A night here would allow for a stroll into Kington the next morning and maybe a look around the famous Hergest Croft Gardens.

The route out of Gladestry on The Offa's Dyke Path is well signposted with the rather superior national trail fingerposts and one is soon up onto the Hergest Ridge. Just past the summit at 426m is the outline of an old racecourse which has a similarity with my home town, where the original Cheltenham racecourse was on Cleeve Hill, and where another national trail, The Cotswold Way passes within a few hundred metres. The descent from this most attractive hill soon meets the aptly named Ridgebourne road and passes the Hergest Croft Gardens to reach the parish church. To the left and behind the church are also a street and house names with Wych derivations. It is then just a nice little stroll down Church Street into this lovely little town.

The alternative and much longer (a day) option, from Builth, gives walkers the opportunity to do another chunk of the WWW and to continue on to Hay on Wye, which is 33.5km. (21m) However there is definitely

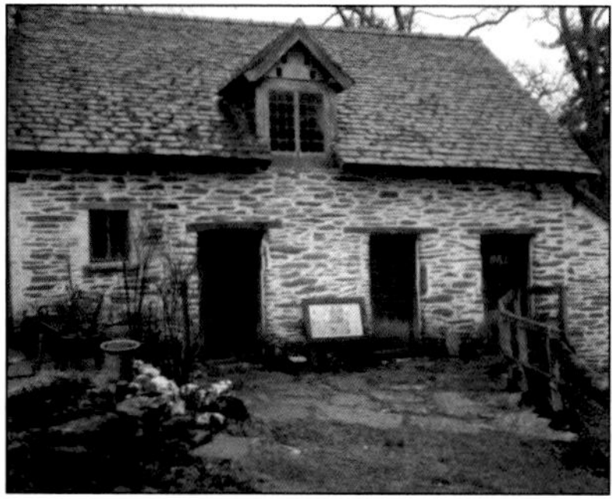

Bothy at Gilfach

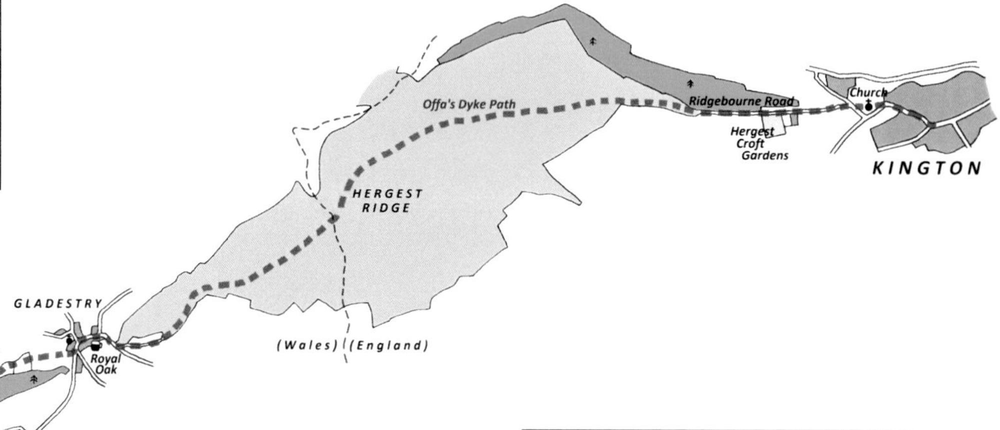
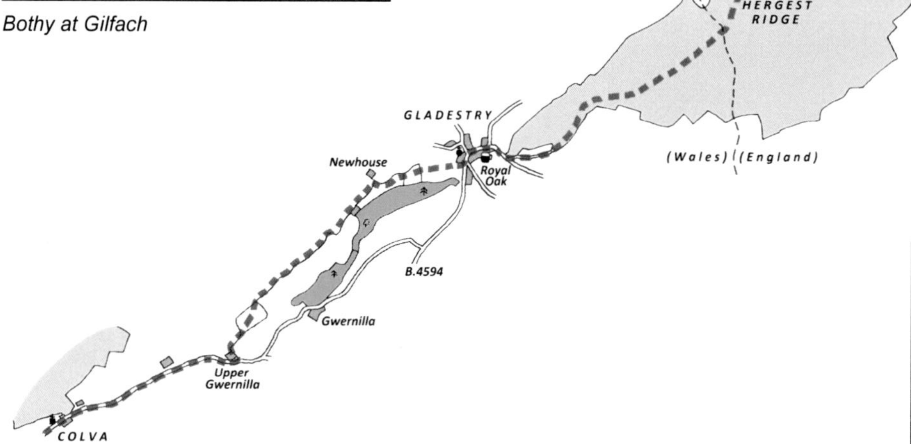

Offa's Dyke Path
Ridgebourne Road
Church
Hergest
Croft
Gardens
KINGTON
HERGEST
RIDGE
GLADESTRY
(Wales)
(England)
Newhouse
Royal
Oak
B.4594
Gwernilla
Upper
Gwernilla
COLVA

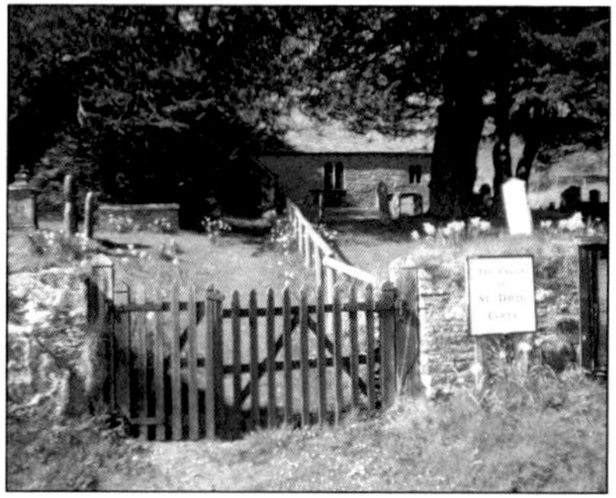

St David's church at Colva

more accommodation along the route and Hay is certainly a lovely place to visit especially if you are like the author a keen book collector! The onward route to Kington is then on The Offa's Dyke path via Gladestry which is a further 23.5km. (14.25m)

THE LONDON CONNECTION
Broadway Tower to Shakespeare's Way
(nr Little Rollright) c30km (19m)

The route from Broadway Tower to the car park at Fish Hill is described at the end of Stage 7 of The Wyche Way but after crossing the main road it is not necessary to go into the car park and to follow the slightly devious route of The Cotswold Way since it is a lot easier to just walk up the minor road for about 200m and join the onward route which then leaves the road on the right. It is only about an hour's walking to Chipping Campden but rather more if you follow the official route up to and around Dovers Hill. The Cotswold Way is full of little! deviations that take in local beauty spots and monuments etc and it just depends on how much of a purist one is for keeping exactly to the official route. Of course, if walkers had previously walked a particular section, it is quite easy to come up with the well known excuse, of having done it before!

Chipping Campden
This is one of the most picturesque Cotswold towns, and since it is not on a main road, it can be quite quiet (at times.) It is a delight to walk around, with many fine buildings emulating back to the 17th century when the wool trade bought prosperity here. There is a good selection of individual shops and a number of fine hotels and pubs. It is definitely important to book any

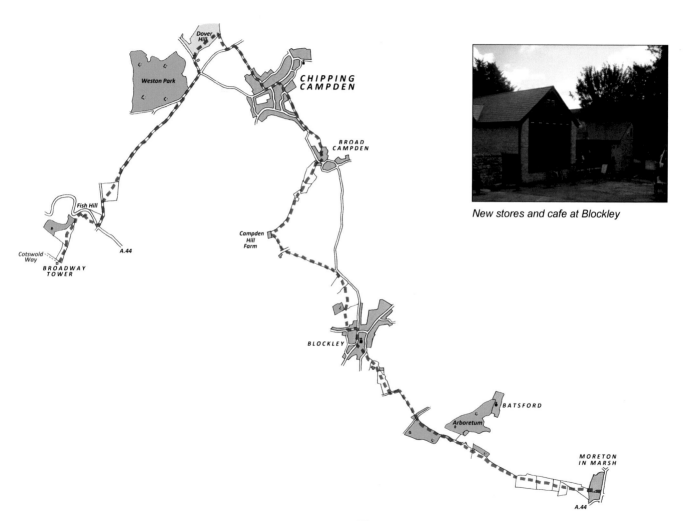

DOVER HILL

Weston Park

CHIPPING CAMPDEN

BROAD CAMPDEN

Fish Hill

A.44

Cotswold Way

BROADWAY TOWER

Campden Hill Farm

BLOCKLEY

BATSFORD

Arboretum

MORETON IN MARSH

A.44

New stores and cafe at Blockley

accommodation in advance and apart from the hotels there are some smaller B&Bs hidden away in the back streets.

The next objective is Moreton in Marsh which is a delightful half day's walk of about 13km (8m). The route follows The Heart of England Walk (HoE) for nearly all the way to Moreton. Leaving Campden is interesting since the route leaves the High Street through the old coaching entrance to The Noel Arms Hotel and then proceeds in a straight line through the outskirts of the town to join a minor road to Broad Campden. Approaching the village one can either continue along the pavement or skirt to the north of the village and turn back into the village past an old Quaker House.

Whichever route is taken, the onward route of the HoE is found on the opposite side of the road, and just to the south of The Bakers Arms pub. The route (SSW) then proceeds to Campden Hill Farm, and then SSE, and S, to the delightful village of Blockley. A deviation into the village centre is really worthwhile since there are not only two pubs, but a really good village shop, and a cafe alongside with all sorts of goodies. Definitely worthwhile stopping here for a mid morning break.

Leaving Blockley can be quite tricky in that one needs to turn down behind the shop and cafe to the churchyard and then exit on to a minor road where turn right. The turning off for the HoE is the second footpath on the left just past Mill Dene Garden. The route then climbs steeply up a long meadow to reach a broad track, where turn left, and shortly after onto a track on the right. The route then proceeds in a straight line SE and passes close to The Batsford estate with its famous arboretum.

An estate entrance road is crossed and then at another junction of paths we carry on ahead whilst the HoE trail goes off to the right. Moreton in Marsh can soon be seen ahead in the distance and after a succession of meadows we enter the town and arrive at the broad and busy High Street.

Moreton in Marsh *came to prominence as a major staging point for coaches on the two old highways which converge on the town, of which The Fosse Way goes back to Roman times. The wide high street has a charter for markets going back centuries and a weekly market is still held today. There are several good hotels and pubs with plenty of accommodation. The town is also on the main Birmingham to London railway line with the station conveniently close to the town centre.*

Unfortunately there is no alternative to continuing our route without sticking close to the A44 Oxford road which we have to do for just over 5km (3miles). There is pavement for nearly the first mile and thereafter there is a good wide verge to walk on. About half way along the road we pass the Four Shires Stone on our left which is now a little out of date since the old Worcestershire boundary is no more, but Gloucestershire, Oxfordshire and Warwickshire still meet here.

About 200m past a turning for Barton on the Hill, you need to look for an obscure stile in the left hand hedge. The path initially goes diagonally left into another field but then proceeds east to join an access road to Salters Well Farm. (the name of the farm comes from a time when this was probably on a Saltway coming down from Droitwich in Worcestershire and proceeding towards Oxford and London) You are now on a bridle way that soon crosses a minor road and then passes Hawton Farm. where one takes a left fork to continue ahead and uphill.

A prominent radio mast will be soon seen up on the skyline, which is our destination, but we have to veer away from this and to follow a boundary hedge on the left before turning back to a minor road where the mast is situated. At this point you have reached Shakespeare's Way, and at the height of about 240 metres it is one of the highest points on the trail. The remote hamlet of Little Rollright with its isolated church is about a kilometre further and Chipping Norton with lots of accommodation, shops, pubs and restaurants is a further five km (3+ miles)

Four Shires stone on A44

78

SHAKESPEARE'S WAY

I think that if I lived in London and wanted to do a long distance trail that was easy going, had plenty of variety, and was easy to access in several stages, I would be tempted to do this one. The start at Stratford upon Avon is attainable by either train or long distance coach and there are a good number of towns on route with transport connections. The whole 146 mile route could also be easily divided into weekends or several longer stages.

There is an excellent guide book which is also subtitled 'a journey of imagination' and this is published by The Macmillan Way Association on behalf of The Shakespeare's Way Association. There is also a separate accommodation guide available.

It is overall 31 miles from Stratford to Chipping Norton which makes for two days good walking although with a late start from Stratford it might be easier in three. The route follows the River Stour for the first 18 miles but the main accommodation in this area would be in the old town of Shipston on Stour which is a little less distance. The main village between here and Chipping Norton is Long Compton and shortly afterwards our route from The Wyche Way is joined on the high ground just before Little Rollright. There is a good regular bus service that operates between Stratford and Chipping Norton, which also passes through Shipston.

Chipping Norton is probably my favourite Cotswold town. I got to know it well in the late '60s and '70s when I was selling timber products to a number of customers in the area. It is certainly less touristy than many other places and has a really nice mix of shops and some good pubs and there is no shortage of accommodation. The locals call it 'Chippy'.

The Cotswolds flatten out somewhat after leaving 'Chippy' It is 27 miles to Oxford and Woodstock makes for a convenient overnight stop at about 15 miles. Just before Woodstock one enters the Blenheim Estate, which is definitely one of the highlights of the SW . The script in the guidebook shows the correct way out of the estate on the (unmarked) public footpath but beware of missing it and arriving at the official entrance since the staff will want to see your pass for which (as a tourist) you should have paid!

Woodstock

This is a very attractive and upmarket Cotswold village. It has all services including a good selection of pubs but accommodation can be expensive here. There are regular bus services to Oxford so that walkers might decide to have two nights accommodation in Oxford where there is more choice.

The route to Oxford soon arrives at the nearby village of Bladon and passes close to the church where Sir

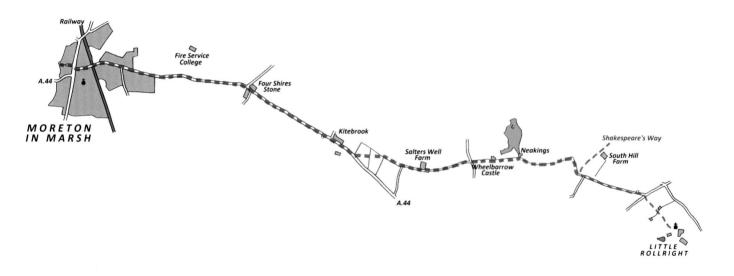

Railway

Fire Service College

A.44

Four Shires Stone

MORETON IN MARSH

Kitebrook

Salters Well Farm

Wheelbarrow Castle

Neakings

Shakespeare's Way

South Hill Farm

A.44

LITTLE ROLLRIGHT

Winston Churchill and many of his family lie buried. There is a later choice of routes into the city centre whereby the slightly longer route follows The Thames Path and passes the attractive Trout Inn at Godstow, whilst the shorter route follows the Oxford canal with hundreds of (many decrepit) barges to pass. The route arrives right in the middle of this very busy city. Walkers booking accommodation should make sure that their B&B is not stuck several miles out in the suburbs.

Oxford

One can hardly do justice to this city (of dreaming spires) in just an evening and it might be worthwhile having a rest day here although most long distance walkers (by and large) regard rest days as superfluous! My recommendations for just a few places to visit would be The Turf Tavern, which is not that far away from Blackwells, the old established booksellers, and a walk around one or two colleges. The greatest thing about walking into and out of the city is that one does not have to bother about car parks or travel tickets so make the best of it!

There is now 37 miles to reach Marlow which is on the River Thames which means either two long days or three reasonable days. The route initially follows the Thames Path down to the small village of Sandford-on-Thames before turning away from the river and making its way on down to The Chilterns which is now

one of my favourite areas to visit. There is not a lot of accommodation around here with Stadhampton one of the larger villages, although only 11 miles from Oxford. Just outside Britwell Salome is the small and attractive town of Watlington but again accommodation is difficult.

You are now definitely in The Chilterns with the beech woods a very attractive feature and Stonor House, with it's lovely parkland, is passed on the way to the attractive village of Hambleden. It is then just five miles or so of delightful woodland walking to reach Marlow where there should be no problem in finding suitable accommodation with plenty of shops, and quite a few good pubs.

It is now 23 miles from Marlow to reach the next significant landmark which is West Drayton where one joins The Grand Union Canal for almost the last stage into central London. The Thames Path is initially followed down to another lovely Thames side village of Cookham, where after, the route heads NE and then SE, down through more lovely woodland walking to Burnham Beeches and then on to Farnham Common where at the A355 there are more shops, pubs and possible accommodation nearby. The route then goes through The Black Country Park and Langley Park to arrive at Iver with more facilities. It is then only a couple of miles after crossing The Slough branch of the Grand Union canal that one arrives at West Drayton with the main line station conveniently nearby. Canal walking is definitely fast and straightforward, but can become a little boring. When I was doing my epic Cape to Cape walk I was able to inform my companion when we reached Devon that it was the 11th canal we had walked along since Scotland. Such is the need for finding useless statistics whilst plodding along the towpath! It is however only 10 miles along the canal before one joins the Thames again at Brentford and there are quite a few locks to pass and lots of chances to converse with all the boat people on route.

The river has now become much larger since we last encountered it some twenty miles back and here one becomes rather divorced from the river traffic. There is now just under thirty miles to go to Shakespeare's Theatre and whilst the walking is very straight forward there are many little deviations around basins and modern developments which have excluded the previous towpath. Bit by bit the skyscrapers in the distance draw nearer and there are interesting buildings and businesses to pass such as ornate rowing clubhouses, Kew Gardens and even Harrods Furniture Depository. The contrast in the different bridges is also interesting, and soon after spotting the Houses of Parliament on the opposite bank, one passes the new and controversial Millennium footbridge, to arrive outside The Globe Theatre.

It has been a journey of much contrast with almost every conceivable style of walking. The Wyche Way is certainly a catalyst for making the whole through route, but for whichever bit walkers decide to do, I hope that they will enjoy the experience.